BEDROCK

BEDROCK

A vision for the local church

David Prior

HODDER AND STOUGHTON
LONDON SYDNEY AUCKLAND TORONTO

British Library Cataloguing in Publication Data

Prior, David
    Bedrock: a vision for the local church.—
    (Hodder Christian paperbacks)
    1. Clergy—Office
    I. Title
    262'.14   BV660.2
    ISBN 0 340 36345 2

To the Church of God which is in Wynberg, Cape Town, South Africa, especially the people of St. John's Parish.

Bedrock, the solid rock under superficial formations: fundamental principles.

Chambers Twentieth Century Dictionary

Acknowledgements

This book originated and grew in daily ministry in two very different parishes – St. John's, Wynberg, in Cape Town between 1972 and 1979, and St. Aldate's in Oxford between 1979 and 1984. Both are reasonably large and active parishes, but there the similarity ends. In both situations we enjoyed the privilege of working out – often painfully and unsuccessfully – God's vision for his Church in that area. The material in the book expresses something of this experience. I want to thank everyone in Cape Town and Oxford who contributed to the book in ways unknown to virtually everyone.

More specifically, my thanks for typing the manuscript go again to Anne Johnson, who has been secretary at St. Aldate's for over ten years – an example of patience and loyalty which is in itself a minor miracle in such a pressurised situation. Otherwise, innumerable friends have in varying ways contributed to forging this book on the anvil of local-church life, especially all with whom I have sought to press back the frontiers of shared leadership. I thank God for this partnership and pray that more churches will discover such ministry.

Contents

Introduction

Over the last fifteen years or so I have had the opportunity of visiting local churches in over twenty different countries, often taking part in special times of evaluation, as Christians have discussed where their church is going and what God wants for it. In the last five years, with the privilege of serving a church in the middle of an international university city like Oxford, I have met hundreds of Christians from local churches all over Britain and, indeed, the world. Frequently the conversation centres on the life of the church near their home. Always they express a genuine concern for its healthy growth, but often there seems to be a lack of direction and vision. Activity usually abounds, although some churches lack even that. Sometimes local churches seem to lose a vision which once gave them purpose and hope – either through complacency, or through sheer tiredness, or through becoming too complicated in both structures and organisation.

This book originated in a thorough search for such a vision from God from one local church in South Africa. In the general turmoil which followed the concentrated violence in the black townships of Soweto in June 1976, the need for God's vision for the church became paramount. Deep bitterness and potential disintegration were nothing new for South Africa, but it has been impossible since Soweto 1976 to ignore or discount the profound shaking which those events depicted.

Universal shaking

In the Third World this shaking is obvious, endemic and inescapable. In recent years it has begun to touch the nerve-ends of sophisticated life in affluent countries. The menace of nuclear war no longer appals only a tiny minority who wear badges, go on marches and picket military bases. If we allow ourselves the freedom to think realistically about the immense vulnerability of life on our planet, it is impossible not to feel the shaking. At times it seems that all our familiar surroundings and securities are being tossed around like a rag doll in the teeth of some immense but invisible hound of hell.

For some time most of us have been able to insulate ourselves from the full fury of this shaking, either by non-exposure to its most naked forces or by the illusion of material securities. But that does not stop the shaking, and increasingly these props are being swept away. The growing spectre of thousands upon thousands of unemployed young people, aimless and hopeless, is becoming almost too oppressive to contemplate. There seems to be no way, in the increasing technology of our generation, by which this trend can be reversed.

If it is true that the world order we have known for so long is being fundamentally shaken, it is not surprising that Christians are looking in their churches for something more stable, yet flexible; more relevant, yet durable; more absorbing, yet fulfilling. Without such "eternal life", i.e. life which comes from and reflects the nature of God himself, we become dull and remote – religious chameleons who change according to our immediate environment, as brittle and as superfluous as everything around us.

It is that kind of bondage to decay and irrelevance that the Bible calls "perishing". The Book of Proverbs indicates that "where there is no vision, the people perish."[1] Many Christians and many local churches are perishing for lack of a vision of what God wants them to be in a precarious world. Some escape into pietistic irrelevance, organising religious meetings and effectively living in a special world which is hermetically sealed from the cosmic shaking all around them – rather like some spiritual antinuclear fall-out shelter where people hide and wait. Many local churches organise themselves in such a way that they effectively end up by becoming ghettoes of escapism; some actually intend and plan to be like that: "here is the ark; come into it and you will be safe."

God the shaker

Late in 1976, in the wake of the Soweto upheaval in South Africa, four Christians in Cape Town – a black South African, a white Englishman, a so-called Cape Coloured and a white South African – spent a week together in a remote cottage in the mountainous hinterland of the Cape. Each individual pursued his private study during the day; in the evenings and over meals we talked endlessly about South Africa, its problems and potential.

In that week I dwelt on particular passages in Hebrews, in an attempt to discern the essential priorities for God's Church in such a tense and fragile situation. Nine unshakeable things seemed to crystallise as the week continued – acceptable worship (12:22–24, 28 and 29; 13:15), love for the brethren (13:1), love for the stranger (13:2), love for the underprivileged (13:3), Christian family life (13:4), a sharing lifestyle (13:5, 6 and 16), shared leadership (13:7 and 17), sound teaching (13:9–11), and shame and suffering (13:12–14).

In Hebrews 12:27 the writer specifically talks of God shaking both the heavens and the earth, i.e. the cosmos or the whole created universe, with the express purpose of removing "what is shaken . . . in order that what cannot be shaken may remain." He urges his readers to "be grateful for receiving a kingdom that cannot be shaken". This kingdom will remain into eternity, outlasting all the apparently permanent world all around us. The realities of God's kingdom have been given to God's people; they are as unshakeable as the King of the kingdom, Jesus Christ who remains "the same yesterday and today and for ever" (13:8). When, therefore, a local church bases its life on these realities, these unshakeable things, it will demonstrate the life of God's kingdom.

When we look at what God is doing with his Church at the end of the twentieth century, internationally but also at the local level, we get the irresistible conviction that he is stripping away cumbersome inessentials, trimming us down to prepare us for battle conditions.

Battle conditions

In his book, *Bursting the Wineskins*, Michael Cassidy writes of a word or prophecy brought to him at a determinative watershed in his calling as a leader of Africa Enterprise (an interracial, interdenominational ministry of evangelism and social involvement). The heart of this message from God was: "There are some shakings that shall come upon you. Yea, everything around you that can be shaken will be shaken, and what remains will be of my Spirit. In the midst of battle, stand still in quietness and peace." Commenting on the importance of these words in ensuing months and years, Michael Cassidy writes: "I was fearful about the shakings. Unbeknown to me, our team was due in the following two years to enter such a set of convulsions as would leave the ministry almost destroyed. During this time of convulsion all I had to hold on to were these prophetic words, plus the accompanying assurance that God was somehow in it all for His purpose. Otherwise I would have given up."[2] Of course, there has always been a war on, and one of the most important spiritual lessons we can learn is to be continuously conscious of this warfare.

When Jesus, the King of kings, began his public ministry on the Palestinian stage two thousand years ago, all other kingdoms began to totter – beginning with Herod's terror when he heard of another King, a baby, in the land. It was not long before the might of Imperial Rome was trembling, ever so menacingly, at the rumour of another King whose subjects faced lions, fire and crucifixion rather than call Caesar Lord. In the pressurised arena of the first century, the followers of Jesus were under no illusions that they were in a battle. In succeeding centuries loyal disciples have always been conscious of fighting a war, not against earthly rulers but "against the principalities, against the powers, against the world rulers of this present darkness, against the spiritual hosts of wickedness in the heavenly places".[3] This spiritual conflict with Satan and his forces was forced out into the open by the public ministry of Jesus, as the Gospel of Mark particularly underlines. Whenever the Spirit of Jesus is moving in similar power, the same clarification of issues takes place.

At the same time there can be little doubt that Jesus's understanding and expression of real power, seen in apparent weakness and abjuring all manipulation and violence, has always distinctively threatened those who wield the greatest worldly authority. The reality of spiritual warfare inevitably intensifies, therefore, when those in power perceive in the Christian Church an authentic manifestation of the kingdom of God. As a local church expresses in its life style the things which cannot be shaken, there will increasingly be confrontation between Church and state. This has always been the mark of a faithful Church. It seems right to make this clear as we look at these nine unshakeable things, because it would be easy to think that they are a recipe for success and happiness, neither of which constitutes God's vision for his Church.

Win . . . train . . . send

This book has one principal purpose. On several occasions in different countries, cultures and congregations I have taken these nine unshakeable things and urged members of a local church to test their whole corporate life by these priorities of the kingdom of God. I suppose it would be fair to say that the responsibility of any church is to win people to Christ, to train them as disciples, and to send them out to serve God amongst their contemporaries. It is my conviction that, by submitting the life of a local church to these nine priorities, it will see more accurately whether it is thus winning, training and sending. There are many congregations which win, but do not train. There are some which win and train, but do not send. There are others which train, but neither win nor send. There are a few which win and send without training. If each local church examined itself to see whether these nine unshakeable things are top of their agenda, we would see the Church everywhere demonstrating "the kingdom which cannot be shaken" in a world that is falling apart. Such self-examination requires a steady but comprehensive investigation of everything that is going on in the life of the Church with a double-edged question in our minds: does each activity express or undermine the unshakeable qualities of the kingdom of God? If something is revealed to be out of alignment, there needs to be a ruthless commitment to what Bill Burnett (formerly Archbishop of Cape Town) has called "planned death".

In most local churches there are activities and organisations which need to die. Their original purpose has long since been forgotten. They have become introverted and self-protective. They do not brook any outside interference. They insist on their right to continue, usually over and above any or all other organisations. Their leadership is often self-perpetuating. The net result is negligible spiritual life of any kind and, at best, a continual process of going through the motions.

At worst, those involved in such groups stifle any creative change which looks like threatening the status quo. This attitude can often be detected in such prosaic details as the church secretary trying to arrange which group holds its meetings in which room on which day at which time. When rivalry between such groups makes such decisions a real headache, it may be time to examine the validity of them all.

One parish in Cape Town faced this kind of situation. For example, there were at least three different groups for women in the church. When we traced the history of each group – i.e. when it started and why – it became plain that competitiveness and keeping up with the ecclesiastical Joneses were very influential factors: other churches had a successful group of this kind, so must we. This desire to impress had continued over the years and it was constantly hitting the surface, especially if there was any hint of evaluation, let alone extinction. The most threatening development of all was any suggested merger or absorption into one gathering.

It is questionable whether it is right for any aspect of a local church's life to continue if its origins lie in such fleshly and worldly motivations. At the very least these powerful dynamics need to be exposed, confessed and renounced. Such a course of action clears the decks for proper and plain guidance from the Holy Spirit for the future. It may be that God will indicate fresh beginnings for such a group on the right foundations. Often the only answer is to let the group die or even to kill it off. Such "euthanasia" often rids a church of the kind of clutter which is preventing real growth.

The good and the best

It is surprising how something that is good, very good, in itself can sometimes block the very best which God wants for a church. Twenty years ago, one of the non-negotiable events in any lively evangelical church was the weekly prayer-meeting. This was virtually the yardstick of true spirituality and effectiveness. It was taught – and it was clearly understood – that the prayer-meeting was the single most important mid-week meeting in the life of the Church. To miss it was a pity; to avoid it was to be "not keen"; to question it was virtual heresy.

I remember well the mild eruption in Cape Town which greeted the proposal that this weekly tryst should be replaced by small home-churches (i.e. "cells" of about a dozen or so meeting in different homes to explore and express what it is to be the Church). I suppose there were about thirty people attending the weekly prayer-meeting. There was nothing trivial or treadmill about these gatherings; so it would be misleading to have seen them as dead and disposable. The need – and the desire – to pray together for the ministry of the Church remained paramount. But it was necessary to step up the quality of pastoral care and personal discipleship if we were not going to level out in our spiritual lives.

Eventually, after a considerable amount of teaching, patient waiting, informal discussion and a weekend retreat, we invited all who so wished to join the proposed home-churches. About twenty people opted in, but the rest decided to stick to the weekly prayer-meeting. We started two home-churches, retained the prayer-meeting and all joined together once a month. Within six months the manifest growth in spiritual vitality amongst those in the two home-churches convinced the uncertain who had remained in the prayer-meeting. The main ingredients of the prayer-meeting (intercession and Bible study) were absorbed (in different formats) into the home-churches, and the parish took several large strides forward as a result.

The process just described is an example of "planned death". It does not have to be either callous or destructive. The three major needs are: first, honestly evaluating a gathering's spiritual pedigree and current condition; secondly, pin-pointing its valued and appreciated ingredients; thirdly, providing these good things in a context which is open to growth, expressive of the rich diversity of life together in the Church, and less prone to being controlled by those with a proprietary attitude to leadership.

In the mid-1970s a similar course of action, though more far-reaching in numbers and impact, was followed in Buenos Aires in the Hidalgo church, pastored at that time by Juan Carlos Ortiz. He was convinced, along with those with him in pastoral leadership, that the Church members needed more opportunity for personal help in Christian discipleship. He divided the church into pastoral units, each under the oversight of an older Christian. This worked, umbrella-fashion, all the way through the congregation. The elders each cared for six or eight people; each of those cared for six or eight; each of those cared for six or eight . . . and so on, until the whole congregation (probably as many as a thousand in 1976, when I visited it) was personally cared for by a Christian older in faith than himself.

Juan Carlos Ortiz gradually implemented this pattern of pastoral care alongside the normal and traditional activities of the Church. Although these were many and various, he did not kill them off. He allowed them to continue. When asked by outsiders what precisely he was doing, he would answer with a Latin twinkle in his eye: "I am building an underground Church. As it grows in health and vitality, the overground Church begins to crack and crumble – because it has no real life. When it finally collapses, the underground Church can come out into the open and become the overground Church."

This is "planned death" in the Latin American style: less sophisticated, more direct than our Cape Town experience – but very effective. Some such ventures are bound to cause a lot of pain and hurt, because it is all too easy to become over-attached to our particular Christian work or group. We find our identity and our fulfilment in what we do for the Lord, not in what he has done for us in Christ. Our work becomes our security, not God's grace. We feel threatened and we lash out when that work is impeded, impugned or investigated because we think that it is a personal attack on our own "kingdom" or even our very selfhood.

It is no bad exercise to allow such a process of exposure to lay bare the quality of our discipleship. Any local church will, if it is honest with the Lord, experience several such moments of truth. Often the crunch will come over money. In at least three of the churches in which I have been involved this has burst out into the open after years of generous giving and careful stewardship. In one such church a financial crisis occurred because a treasurer was elected whose financial acumen was considerable but whose Christian commitment and personal ethics were questionable. In another church, the treasurer's Christian commitment was clear but a serious weakness in handling money became apparent only after the embezzlement of large amounts of church funds.

In these cases the congregations concerned had allowed secular considerations to override spiritual priorities, and had entrusted responsibility to the treasurer without proper pastoral care for him as a whole person. This wholeness (the essence of the biblical doctrine of salvation) is God's will for each local church as well as for each individual Christian. Indeed, as individuals we find wholeness only within the developing wholeness of our local church. As we evaluate our churches in the light of these nine characteristics of God's eternal kingdom – and particularly as we take note of what might require some sensitive euthanasia – we can have confidence that in God's will is our peace, our "shalom", our wholeness. In discovering and doing that will we may be hurt and meet much pain, but we will gradually become like Christ – which is what matters.

A time to evaluate

One word of caution is always necessary when embarking on a process of evaluation. It is as dangerous to do it too often as to refuse ever to do it. The little boy who is constantly digging up his seeds to see whether they are still growing is proverbial. Many Christians, including those entrusted with oversight in local churches, are too prone to conducting evaluations rather than too reluctant. The overall atmosphere in such churches is one of being constantly checked out rather than of being trusted with real responsibility. The sieve seems to be continuously raking through this activity and that meeting, this project and that task.

Growth takes time. It is not for nothing that most of the biblical metaphors for growth are taken from nature. The seasons of the year have their counterpart in the life of local churches. Seeds are planted – and hidden – in winter. They spring up and out in glad but vulnerable new life. Summer sees a blaze of colour and vegetation. Autumn is a time of fruitfulness and quiet enjoyment of God's bounty. Then winter gradually strips away most visible signs of growth, but also provides a quiet opportunity for rest, recuperation and fresh sowing. A graph of the spiritual life of a local church would reveal similar patterns.

There is, therefore, a time to evaluate and a time to press on without evaluating. For many readers of this book it may well not be appropriate to hold up the life of their church to such rigorous scrutiny. For others that time is overdue: the ground must be turned over. For every church there will be the right time.

Some years ago in Oxford we were involved in such evaluation. Apart from other specific details, the main lesson we learned then was the need to *prune* our activities, to give space and thus to facilitate more growth at the appropriate time. The command to prune was illustrated by several pictures (received in corporate times of prayer) of sprawling plants, bushes, trees, shrubs – I remember one of a rose-bush, another of a vine. There was one clear message – prune or shrivel.

But perhaps the most telling point of all was the reminder that the Lord is the vine-dresser, not the members or the leaders of a local church. The divine Gardener, amongst other activities, prunes the Church. If any of its activities are unfruitful, he gets out his secateurs. Most "planned death" is, therefore, cheerful co-operation with God – indeed, it may well be that *all* "planned death" must be undertaken as willing involvement in God's pruning work. If God has his knife into a cherished activity or organisation, we will be most foolish to hang on to it. It will die anyway.

When, therefore, it is right to evaluate the life of your church, make unhurried time to do so; let those involved get away from home territory into a "retreat" atmosphere; do not put too much on the agenda at any one gathering; create an atmosphere in which all can listen to God. Such an event needs to avoid the urgency of the immediate and the narrowness of the particular: for example, if the nine unshakeable things of Hebrews 12 and 13 become valuable touchstones of your life together as the family of God, do not point the searchlight at one or two recent church services, but at attitudes and priorities in worship. If evangelism is on the agenda, look at the way Christians are spending their time and the nature of their friendship with outsiders, not at the last guest service. If the concern is teaching and training, investigate the way the content of sermons is digested and put into practice, rather than the next sermon series.

Naturally, specifics and particulars will illustrate the matter under discussion – but, very often, such evaluation never gets off the ground because people tend to argue about nitty-gritty details. This is very plain when worship is under review. Understandably, personal sensitivities and preferences are most keenly felt on this issue. If, however, we can allow a true biblical understanding of what worship is – and why we worship – to control our thinking and decision-making, we will gradually be liberated from endless debates about tunes, length of services, types of music, etc.

Now that we have pleaded the case for proper evaluation in the life of a local church, and at the same time pointed out some of the pitfalls along the route, it is time to look at the first of these nine unshakeable things in the kingdom of God.

1   Acceptable worship

"Therefore let us be grateful for receiving a kingdom that cannot be shaken, and thus let us offer to God acceptable worship, with reverence and awe."[1]

It is a sad, but accurate, commentary on much of our Church life that the English words "worship" and "service" have been reduced to church notice-boards, advertising specific times when there will (always) be a "service" of "worship". Worship is the eternal activity of the life of heaven. It is the highest calling and privilege of mankind. It is the constant delight of the heavenly host. Two familiar hymns, from very different traditions, describe the experience when "we lose ourselves in heaven above"[2] and of being "lost in wonder, love, and praise".[3]

Can our regular Sunday services be described in those terms? Does such worship motivate our life together as the people of God? Do our decisions and our programmes take their cue from such worship? Is worship at the heart of our fellowship and policy-making? There are few aspects of local church life which need more radical reassessment and more thorough overhaul. Earlier (page 13) I explained the relevance of the last two chapters of Hebrews. Those chapters provide us with some searching insights into worship which is genuinely acceptable to God (12:28). Here are six: acceptable worship touches eternity (12:22–24); is directed towards God (12:28); is fired by gratitude (12:28); is controlled by reverence and awe (12:28 and 29); is the fruit of consistent living (13:15); is a sacrifice (13:15) – it would be helpful to have the text of Hebrews in front of you.

1   Acceptable worship touches eternity (Heb. 12:22–24)

The writer gives a remarkable panorama of what is happening when God's people come together to worship him. Often we are hemmed in by all too tangible factors in congregational worship, factors which lock us into very human and earthly realities like robes and hats, tunes and books, instruments and pews. We need the corrective of these verses, which remind us that we have come, as Christians, "to Mount Zion and to the city of the living God, the heavenly Jerusalem".[4]

Under the old covenant it was an exhilarating experience to join the crowds of pilgrims arriving after their (often lengthy) journey to Jerusalem for one of the great festivals of the Jews. This fiesta experience is to be the continuous experience of God's people gathered together, a time of expectancy: the living God is there in the midst in a special way – "where two or three are gathered together in My name," affirmed Jesus, "there am I in the midst of them."[5]

Many of the psalms express this joyful exuberance, not least when they reflect the desperate longing produced by enforced and prolonged absence from temple worship. For example, the first two verses of Psalm 84: "How lovely is thy dwelling place, O Lord of hosts! My soul longs, yea, faints for the courts of the Lord; my heart and flesh sing for joy to the living God." The psalmist recognises the supreme joy of those who spend their days in such worship: "Blessed are those who dwell in thy house, ever singing thy praise! . . . For a day in thy courts is better than a thousand elsewhere. I would rather be a doorkeeper in the house of my God than dwell in the tents of wickedness."[6]

With a laudable desire to switch our focus from holy places to the inner shrine of the heart, we have often missed out on the excitement and the satisfaction of God's people coming together for worship. It might be revealing to ask ourselves whether we actually miss such corporate worship when we are prevented from attending – perhaps through illness, travel or holidays. Do we long to experience the presence of the Lord in this way? The psalmist experienced the holiness and sovereignty of God in a distinctive way in the midst of people gathered for worship: "Thou art holy, enthroned on the praises of Israel."[7]

David articulated this longing eloquently in Psalm 27: "One thing have I asked of the Lord, that will I seek after; that I may dwell in the house of the Lord all the days of my life, to behold the beauty of the Lord, and to inquire in his temple."[8] On several occasions he describes his desire to join in the worship of "the great congregation" not as a passive observer but as an active participant. He wants to add his personal song of praise for God's active deliverance when in deep trouble – "then I will thank thee in the great congregation; in the mighty throng I will praise thee."[9]

Once granted such deliverance, he hastened to tell his fellow-believers: "I have told the glad news of deliverance in the great congregation; lo, I have not restrained my lips, as thou knowest, O Lord. I have not hid thy saving help within my heart, I have spoken of thy faithfulness and thy salvation; I have not concealed thy steadfast love and thy faithfulness from the great congregation."[10]

When he was cut off from such opportunities for public worship, the psalmist found himself hankering after its fulfilling joy: "These things I remember, as I pour out my soul: how I went with the throng, and led them in procession to the house of God, with glad shouts and songs of thanksgiving, a multitude keeping festival."[11] Many of the psalms actually ascribed to David seem to have been written in times of desolation and depression, when he was cut off from such worship. One such is Psalm 63 where, "in a dry and weary land where no water is",[12] David seeks God directly by remembering: "I have looked upon thee in the sanctuary, beholding thy power and glory."[13] In one of the many psalms dedicated to "the choirmaster" in charge of this public worship, David declares: "Blessed is he whom thou dost choose and bring near, to dwell in thy courts! We shall be satisfied with the goodness of thy house, thy holy temple."[14]

It is important to allow the full significance of that last statement to sink in. David knew nothing of God's grace as expressed fully and visibly in Jesus Christ. His experience of forgiveness and of the fullness of God's Spirit were inevitably partial and temporary. Yet he found the worship of the temple absolutely central to his faith. It was thus central because it was deeply satisfying – and perhaps it deeply satisfied him because he made it central.

So much public worship today is not satisfying. There is great reward in examining the psalmists' worship because (apart from the sacrificial system on which the temple worship was based, which has been replaced by a far richer and complete sacrifice in the death of Jesus) all its elements and ingredients are available to us today. Here are some of them, taken at random from the psalms: recounting personal answers to prayer; returning to give thanks; paying our vows to God; jubilant exultation with all kinds of instruments (the loud, the plaintive, the rhythmic); solemn and stately processions; personal testimony; celebration in dance; spontaneous thank-offerings; reciting God's wonderful deeds over the years and the centuries; crying out to God for protection, guidance, rescue and forgiveness; quiet meditation on the sheer goodness of the Lord; composing and singing personal songs of praise and faith. It is no surprise that David exclaims; "Bless God in the great congregation, the Lord, O you who are of Israel's fountain."[15]

If we look again at the titles to many of the psalms, and then imaginatively apply their content to their context, we can see the key factor of personal involvement by each individual as he or she brings that heart-felt contribution to the worship of God's gathered people.

All these factors point to the need of the local church to give more time, imagination, effort and prayer to the public worship. There is a deep sense of satisfaction in such worship, because in it God ministers to us as whole people. Such true and acceptable (as distinct from purely cerebral) worship is the means for God's grace to touch us intellectually, emotionally and spiritually. Anybody who has, even spasmodically, experienced this will know that such deep satisfaction is available nowhere else on earth, precisely because in it we touch eternity. And, paradoxically but as we might expect, this touch of eternity, this taste of heaven, sends us back into the world ready to press forward as committed citizens of the kingdom of God. If we are deprived of such satisfying worship, our hold on things eternal is extremely shaky.

God's people, redeemed by the precious blood of Christ and indwelt by God's Holy Spirit, will be satisfied with nothing less than such worship. The particular emphasis of the phrase "acceptable worship" in Hebrews 12:28 falls on its being acceptable *to God*. All Christians – and most fringe-adherents – have very strong views about what is acceptable at the personal level in the worship services of a local church. We need to listen far less to the opinions of human beings and concentrate on the eternal and Godward aspects of worship.

If the worship in a church touches eternity in this way, many of the complaints and problems which loom so large in its life will assume proper proportions – not least because the worship will spill over into and form an essential part of everything else which takes place, whether in decision-making, in personal discipleship or in daily routine.

Expectancy

For these reasons it is important in the Church to foster a genuine sense of expectancy in approaching public worship: God is in the midst of us, and things are going to happen, people are going to be changed. That will inevitably mean that those responsible for leading worship on behalf of God's people cannot do less than spend twenty minutes or so together in prayer and praise before a service begins. In Oxford we have done this for four years or more, and it has indisputably increased the mood of quiet expectancy in the Sunday services. Clergy, those leading the music, those administering the bread and wine at Holy Communion, all with any part to play in the service (sometimes as many as thirty) gather in the upper room – including anyone who wants to give out a notice. In this way we find we can sensitise one another to the living God – and that means leaving others with suitable gifts to welcome the congregation and to do any last-minute business which needs to be done.

Clergy are very prone to rushing off to see one last person before the service begins, thus creating a sense of dis-ease when there should be peace and a quiet looking to God. Usually this trend indicates bad organisation as well as wrong priorities. Often it reveals the need for the administration to be taken out of the hands of the clergyman altogether, so that he has no need to be distracted from the awesome responsibility of leading the people of God in worship.

If such worship is going to happen more than once in a blue moon, it is clear that an immense responsibility falls on all committed to leadership of such services. A number of small suggestions may prove helpful at this point. We have concluded that leading worship is too onerous a responsibility for one person to carry alone. Attention should be given to providing easy communication between such people as the leader of the service, the preacher, the organist or music director, and anybody else at the heart of the worship. These three or four people can then sense together the moving of the Spirit in any service – and respond accordingly. Such a team, incidentally, needs to be consistently the same (with the odd exception) if the congregation as a whole is to develop a relaxed confidence in the leadership of its worship. Constant change – of personnel and of content – creates restlessness, confusion and anxiety.

This kind of shared approach to leading worship also releases far more congregational participation. It is valuable to encourage such participation by guided times of waiting quietly in God's presence, expecting different members of the congregation to contribute in any of the different ways mentioned in 1 Corinthians 14:26 – a hymn, a lesson, a revelation, a tongue or an interpretation. One of the releasing factors here is the freedom to make mistakes. If, for example, someone starts up a suitable song or hymn, but in the wrong key (too high or too low), it is not a disaster. It can often be remedied unostentatiously by a deft touch from a more musical person, either on a piano or organ or guitar or *a cappella* (i.e. unaccompanied voice).

Angels

Hebrews 12:22 unveils the inspiring fact that another congregation is present when God's people gather together – "innumerable angels in festal gathering". We have, generally speaking, lost the sense of angelic beings present with us in worship, and we are impoverished as a result. The angels cannot, apparently, appreciate the glories of God's salvation – according to Peter,[16] they long to investigate what it means to be "ransomed, healed, restored, forgiven",[17] but, not having known sin, they cannot appreciate forgiveness. Nevertheless they love God and spend eternity adoring him.[18] The multitudes of this heavenly host are present in our worship, even if it is actually only two or three people gathered in that one place. They are not merely present as worshippers; they are present in order to make our worship "take off": for "are they not all ministering spirits sent forth to serve, for the sake of those who are to obtain salvation?"[19]

But there is yet another "church" present when the local congregation gathers to worship God according to the writer of the Hebrews – "the Church (the Greek word literally is 'ecclesia') of the first-born, which are written in heaven".[20] Clearly the writer is convinced that the local church at worship in some way joins the universal Church in every generation in one great communion of saints. There can be few Christians who have not at some stage touched the fringes of this glorious experience, when praise and adoration have somehow opened a window into eternity, and we have been conscious of something richer, fuller, freer and infinitely greater.

The first-born

The reference to "the first-born, which are written in heaven" emphasises the need for Christian worship to be led, encouraged, deepened and shared by those who know what it is to be "born from above"[21] by the Spirit of God. If acceptable worship is one unshakeable quality of the Kingdom of God, and if we have to be born again to see and to enter that Kingdom, then it is obvious that those who are not spiritually reborn cannot fully experience true Christian worship. In any gathering of Christian people there will presumably be a few who, as in first-century Corinth, occupy "the position of an outsider":[22] but the substantial majority of Christian worshippers will be those born again by the Spirit of God, and to whom the same Spirit has given an inner assurance that their names are written in the Lamb's book of life,[23] i.e. enrolled in heaven.

Another perspective on this immense congregation which we join when we meet together for Christian worship is provided by the phrase, "just men made perfect".[24] Here the writer holds before us the consummation of God's work in his people, whereby he not only calls men and women to himself but steadily works in them by his Spirit until they become like his Son, Jesus Christ. In Christian worship, we touch the edges of what we are called to be in Christ. We catch a glimpse of our true and eternal purpose in the mind of God. This is enshrined in the words of the song: "Royal sons of a royal King, made to worship, made to praise; kings and priests to the King of kings, made to worship him."[25]

When we have been caught up in this kind of worship, we must have known that this must be what it is like in heaven. We do not want it to stop. Time stands still because we have tasted eternity. We know deep down that this is what we are meant – and always have been meant – to do. In such an experience of worship the eternal purposes of God, from creation through redemption to glory, are compressed into a foretaste of heaven. We touch eternity.

The tyranny of time

When a church's worship fails to reach this quality, the most common reason is the tyranny of time. We have probably grown accustomed to congregations where folk seem to take regular, highly suggestive, glances at their watches. The age of the digital alarm has made the presence of Time even more oppressive. If worship is, by definition, the life of heaven, then we know we have begun to worship "in Spirit and truth"[26] when we lose track of time. When we truly lose ourselves in worship and praise, three hours pass like a flash.

Naturally, different cultures have different expectations and traditions, but true worship transcends the limitations of cultural norms – a fact brought home to me on numerous occasions in Africa and Latin America, where time is not the despot we have managed to make it in the West. Especially in multiracial services of worship in Cape Town, there was an uplifting sense of touching both the timelessness and the internationalism of heaven. Are there not ways of teaching one another to see acceptable worship as more important than the Sunday meal, the imminent visitors, the car and the garden, etc., etc? Is it not of supreme worth thus to touch eternity?

It may well be that the most effective way to introduce a congregation to worship less hampered by time restrictions is away from home territory. Like most new experiences, such worship cannot really be explained by mere words: it needs to be shared. Often this happens most easily and naturally in a weekend away or in a visit to another church or on a parish holiday, or on some other informal occasion. In such settings there is usually no cut-off point or at least no pressing engagements which have, over the years, become like the law of the Medes and Persians, "which altereth not".

I remember well the first occasion when our united (five churches) parish in Cape Town experienced such timeless worship in the actual church building. Strangely enough, it was in a very formal setting indeed: the Archbishop was inducting me as Rector of the parish. In many ways what happened was not organised, let alone engineered, by any human agency: quite simply, God came in and took over. The service began at 7 p.m. and ended at 9.45 p.m., and the time was not even noticed by the thousand or so, of all ages and races, present in the church.

At another level, however, there was something inherent in that situation which was probably very significant. It was a special occasion. For most people it was an unprecedented occasion. There were no tramlines to follow, although it was a service which followed a clear liturgical format. I doubt whether anyone present had planned another engagement that evening. The time had been set apart for God, as an act of celebration. There was an air of expectancy and God surpassed our expectations. In fact, the experience of that single service opened up an approach to worship throughout the parish which was arguably to be the biggest single factor in its spiritual life and growth in the next few years. The clock no longer ruled. The mould had been broken. A substantial majority of the worshipping members of the parish had tasted something different. For a long time the freedom thus released created immense space for many new things to emerge in the church, in its weekly services in traditional buildings, not just in more informal settings where there had already been much new vitality over the preceding six months.

Whatever events God may choose to take as special catalysts for renewing the worship of a local church, the fundamental point at issue remains that of our expectations. If we expect God to move in our worship together Sunday by Sunday, he will – and he will, as always, transcend our expectations.[27] He delights to surprise us all the time, but he particularly loves to do so in showing his "glory in the Church".[28] We are often in danger of illustrating the truth of the unpalatable beatitude: "Blessed is he who expects nothing, for he shall never be disappointed."

One rider is necessary: our expectations must be placed firmly in God himself, not in any human being or human contribution. Disillusionment sets in very easily in local churches because we look to men and not to God. In this priority the message of Psalm 62 is most pertinent, crystallised in this statement of David's: "For God alone my soul waits in silence, for my hope is from him."[29] Usually the most effective way of ensuring that our attention is focussed on God is actually the simplest – i.e. telling everyone to forget about themselves and everyone else and to concentrate on God.

I am often struck – and saddened – by the casual, if not totally uninvolved, way in which Christians approach the act of worship. I remember being first hit by this when, as a young Christian, I was actively involved in a very lively parish church, in which the vicar seemed to spend the whole of the first hymn looking round at the congregation to see who was there. It may have been due to a good pastoral heart, but it did not exactly indicate absorption in worship.

Frequently now I have to stop when I catch myself slipping into the same habit. It is, in fact, purely a matter of concentration. My wife would not think very much of me if, in talking about her virtues and qualities – let alone in telling her directly how much I appreciated her – I was actually looking around at everyone else, thinking about them. One of the most happy and frequent discoveries I am making in worship is the richness of the words in many of our most familiar hymns. To call this a discovery is to reveal how often I have sung them without truly concentrating on the words. That is a rather frightening fact and I am fairly sure that most Christians are similarly guilty.

This matter of concentration needs more investigation. One very simple step would be to arrive at church fifteen minutes earlier and to use the time before the service for preparation. In such a time, many of our distractions can be surrendered to the Lord instead of rushing in at the last moment (or after it) and carrying our anxieties and other preoccupations through the entire service. One of the perverse aspects of our time-ridden culture is that we leave virtually everything to the last moment – and then get impatient if we are delayed.

If those responsible for leading services of worship can discipline themselves by means of twenty minutes' preparation in prayer, it is not too much to ask a congregation similarly to get ready for worship. Many congregations are invisible five minutes before the start of a service, but present in large numbers six or seven minutes later: is this helping concentration on the Lord?

This personal concentration on the Lord by each individual worshipper actually nips in the bud the common complaint about being distracted by what others may be wearing, doing or looking like. It can indeed be distracting if some people lift their hands in worship, and it can be more than distracting if someone is singing loudly out of tune in the pew behind. No doubt both liberated handlifters and discordant boomers need to restrain themselves at times out of sensitivity for others: in a loving community they can be urged to do so. But is it really impossible to concentrate on the Lord in such circumstances? Will the circumstances ever be ideal or perfect this side of heaven? If we want to concentrate and cannot do so (for whatever reason), let us ask God to help us: he will certainly do so if our desire is to worship him in Spirit and in truth.

One of the privileges of being at the front, facing the congregation, in our worship at Oxford is the opportunity to watch the faces (in particular) of the children, who sit on the carpet before the central dais. It is immensely rewarding to watch the faces of these children when they are caught up in praise, or locked in concentration on worship expressed in dance. That concentration helps me to worship God. There have been a number of occasions as well when I have paused in my own singing simply to watch the faces of those "lost in wonder, love and praise". This happened most recently at the end of a televised service, when we had just gone "off the air" and were singing a powerful song of worship. This is the horizontal ministry of worship: as we individually concentrate our gaze on the Lord, so we are all mutually built up by one another.

2   Acceptable worship is directed towards God (Heb. 12:28)

One of the most important weekly activities I take part in is when three or four of us spend an hour or more looking at the form and content of next Sunday's services of worship. Many interesting lessons about acceptable worship have emerged over several years of doing this kind of preparation. One fascinating fact has become clear: much of our worship, especially the more fixed parts of the services and in particular the more traditional hymns, is an objective statement of truths about God, rather than a personal address to God.

Now there is an important place for such strong declaration of what God has done, who he is and what he is like. Paul urges the Ephesians to recognise God's purpose that "through the Church the manifold wisdom of God might now be made known to the principalities and powers in the heavenly places."[30] Whenever we proclaim the mighty acts of God in creation and redemption, we are letting every created being, human and angelic, know the wisdom and the majesty of God. But that is proclamation, not adoration, and acceptable worship is directed towards God.

Adoration

The Book of Revelation has many examples of worship in heaven; more often than not, the words used by worshippers are directed personally to God, e.g. "Worthy art thou, our Lord and God, to receive glory and honour and power, for thou didst create all things, and by thy will they existed and were created."[31] When statements about God's greatness and salvation are made, the context invariably describes the worshippers directing their gaze and their adoration towards God.[32]

If, as has been often pointed out, the meaning of the original Greek word for worship is "to draw near to kiss", we will find it most helpful to address God directly and personally – particularly in psalms, hymns and spiritual songs as much as in the prayers of intercession. On many occasions I have personally felt uneasy during intercession in a congregation because so much of the verbal prayer seems to be aimed horizontally in an almost preaching style. This uneasiness has recently widened to include any occasion when, for whatever reason, there is a marked reluctance actually to speak or sing personally to God.

Paul emphasises the same truth in writing about the worship by the Christian community at Colossae: "Let the word of Christ dwell in you richly, teach and admonish one another in all wisdom, and sing psalms and hymns and spiritual songs with thankfulness in your hearts to God."[33] He here recognises the need for mutual ministry through teaching, but he also stresses ministering to God "in our hearts". We probably all know the need to break through our own feelings – or lack of them – in order to concentrate fully on God in our inner being. In a parallel passage Paul talks about "singing and making melody to the Lord with all your heart",[34] and the context indicates that he regards such worship as one of the results and evidences of being "filled with the Spirit".[35]

There is clearly a place, according to Paul, for mutual encouragement to worship in the congregation, just as there is a proper place for proclamation of the greatness of God as an incentive to worship. But worship itself is directed towards God, to "a Judge who is God of all".[36] We need to encourage one another both to focus on God as we gather for worship, and to tell God personally how much we love him, honour him and want to serve him. When we are in the presence of somebody we love, we certainly want to tell others how much we think of that person – but even more we want to say "I love you" to him/her. There is something lacking in worship which never gets round to saying "I love you" to the one who, above all human beings, has won the love of our hearts and lives.

It may be important actually to ask *why* we sometimes find it difficult to say to the Lord directly, "I love you." For some Christians such a form of address seems out of place, almost irreverent. There are those who find it difficult and embarrassing to say those words to anyone, even the person they love most dearly. Of course, this blockage need not be any indicator of their love for that person.

On the other hand, it can often be true that we have not allowed the Lord to reach that depth in our inner being. The cost of letting him touch our emotions or our memories is too great. We keep his love for us at arm's length, and we may well keep others at a distance as well. To be loved is to be vulnerable; to say "I love you" to another person, even to God, is also to be vulnerable. It may well be, therefore, that there is a degree of superficiality in some people's relationship with God and with others, when any personal expression of love in words is difficult, if not impossible.

Equally, of course, it is easy to use those high-value words very flippantly: to say "I love you" without any depth or appreciation. Many Christians react against this kind of superficial devotion and, in understandably rigorous self-criticism, will not take such words on their lips unless they find they can truly mean them from their hearts. In any case, it is argued, love is a matter of action not words: what, they say, is the point of simply saying them? I suppose the proper answer to this approach is to recall Jesus's own words to Simon Peter on the beach after his resurrection, "Simon, son of John, do you love me?"[37] Three times Jesus asked the same question; three times Peter replied, "I love you."[38] For Peter, who had denied he ever knew Jesus, it was necessary to put his love into words. Perhaps we have not behaved like Peter; perhaps we have, and perhaps we actually behave like him regularly, every week . . . and it may be that the

risen Lord wants regularly in our corporate worship to
hear each of his disciples saying again, "I love you,
Lord."

It may, then, be not reserve or integrity or culture
which holds us back from such love songs as much as
pride in refusing to become like little children, to admit
where we have only recently failed to demonstrate our
love for Jesus, and to make ourselves vulnerable again to
the love of God.

Those who are unaccustomed to such personal expression of love to God find themselves deeply moved in
a congregation which is "lost in wonder, love and
praise". They may not be able to explain their feelings,
except with rather ordinary statements like "You all seem
to mean it." But the real presence of God breaks through
to religious professional and rank outsider alike when
God is being worshipped and adored in this direct way.

I well remember a Sunday morning in Oxford when we
were looking at Paul's magnificent exposition of the
Cross at the end of Romans 3. Half-an-hour's preaching
had clearly gripped the congregation intellectually and
emotionally with the sheer grace of God in Jesus Christ.
The normal ending would have been: "We will now sing
Hymn 246, during which our offertory will be received" – plus the Benediction. But it seemed totally
wrong and inadequate just to say "Amen" to the sermon
and disappear. Instead we suggested that those who
wanted to stay and worship God for his great salvation
should feel free to do so. About 90 per cent of the
congregation stayed, and that time of worship lasted for
another thirty spontaneous minutes. We seem so often to
miss out on acceptable and deeply satisfying worship
simply because we find it hard to move from the objectiv-
ity of "How good is the God we adore" to the love song
"Father, we love you, we worship and adore you."

Buildings and barriers

If worship is to be directed towards God, we need to ask
some fairly leading questions about the buildings in

which we meet as a congregation. By and large, the very
architecture constitutes a crippling drawback. Long, narrow, high buildings, filled with pews are a contradiction
of all the Bible teaches about the Church as a worshipping
community. Particularly in churches designed with the
pulpit dominating everything in the middle at the front,
the people are forced to look at the minister throughout
the "service of worship" – or to close their eyes. Such a
human focus, forced upon God's people at worship by
sheer architecture, has not been noticeably redirected
even in the trends of modern church design, in spite of a
marked tendency to "worship-in-the-round". We need a
bevy of imaginative, converted, biblically-based
architects, who know what acceptable worship is. We
also need the odd earthquake, fire, expropriation and
other "acts of God"!

If such changes are beyond the reach of most local
churches because of inherited buildings, we can still ask
ourselves whether the way we conduct worship actually
directs people to God – or to some human being,
whether that is the priest/minister, the choir, the elders
or the preacher. Granted the need for proper control and
for enabling the leadership of worship, we can still do
much to encourage the congregation to look to the risen
Lord in the midst of his people.

During some oppressively sultry weather in the summer of 1983, it was fascinating to discover what incidental
blessings were released when those leading the services
at our church in Oxford were in shirt-sleeves for an
evening eucharist. Several people commented on the
sense of being the family of God looking to him as Father.
Of course, less formal and liturgically-based congregations operate in this way every week – although there is a
subtle way in which the worship of such fellowships can
still be man-centred, as certain individuals are looked to
for the right contributions and inspiration.

There are other small ways in which a congregation can
be directed towards God in its worship. From time to
time, for example, I have sat with my wife in the body of
the church rather than in the usual place at the front. It

has been noticeable that members of the congregation relate to me at the end of a service quite differently from when I am responsible for leading. Instead of coming to me as a problem-solver, they relate far more as equals along lines such as "What has God said to you tonight?"

3 Acceptable worship is fired by gratitude (Heb. 12:28)

The little word "thus" in Heb. 12:28 refers back to the phrase near the beginning of the verse: "let us be grateful". It is in gratitude that we offer to God acceptable worship. The root word in the Greek text is *charis*, or "grace". God's grace is the mainspring of our gratitude. We have received a kingdom which cannot be shaken and this is God's gift to us in a tottering world. We can indeed be grateful, and such gratitude will spontaneously call forth our worship.

Eucharistic worship

The Greek word *charis* is also at the heart of the "Eucharist", a word which means "Thanksgiving" and is a most suitable word for the Holy Communion service or the Lord's Supper. Like most evangelicals of my vintage, I was brought up on what, frankly, was not just a low view of the value of the Eucharist but a prejudiced, played-down, reactionary attitude. What was seen as the *proper* interpretation of the Holy Communion, as definitely distinct from improper views, was plainly taught – that we are remembering the basis of our salvation in the once-for-all historic death of Jesus. But its value as a means of grace abounding from God to sinners was seriously neglected. The Eucharist was seen, not as the heart of true worship, but as an optional extra, usually tagged on in a quick twenty minutes at the end of the main services of Morning and Evening Prayer. If you were really keen, or wanted to get your Sunday worship

out of the way early in the day, you went to the 8 a.m.
Communion service, which continues steadily in most
Anglican churches all over the world.

Increasingly today, evangelical Christians are catching
up with the rest of Christendom in rediscovering the
centrality of the Eucharist in the worshipping life of the
Church. It is, after all, the only "form of service" which
our Lord himself not merely suggested but enjoined
upon his people. The evidence of the Acts of the Apostles
(and of early Church history in general) strongly indicates that the first Christians enjoyed this form of sac-
ramental worship whenever they met together, which
(according to Luke)[39] was every day. Our own worship
may well remain less than acceptable so long as it does
not enshrine the death of Christ as the ground of our
enjoyment of God's salvation. There is nothing like
absorbing the significance of Christ's death on the Cross
for deepening in us a sense of profound gratitude for
God's sheer goodness in giving us eternal life in his Son.

To those who still warn against the dangers of frequent
celebration I can simply say that this has not proved true
in my own experience. Not only are there many different
ways of sharing in this sacrament – from the most formal
and magnificent to the most spontaneous and instinctive – but there are also inexhaustible veins of spiritual
gold to be mined in exploring the richness of Christ's
death for us.

Furthermore, over the last twelve years or so (since I
began to make the Eucharist more central in my own life)
it has been demonstrated time and time again that
eucharistic worship "has something" which other
worship does not. One of the ingredients most obviously
present is gratitude for God's grace, an ingredient which
the writer to the Hebrews himself brings forcibly to our
attention when he reminds us, "You have come . . . to
Jesus, the mediator of a new covenant, and to the sprink-
led blood that speaks more graciously than the blood of
Abel."[40] Even those phrases afford insights into the
meaning of Christ's death which would not normally or
naturally absorb our thinking about the Cross of Jesus in

less, rather than more, frequent participation in the Eucharist.

There are other, less crucial, ways of allowing gratitude to fire our worship. Opportunities for people to share what God has done for them in the last week, particularly in answer to specific prayer, will often unlock a spirit of thanksgiving amongst the congregation as a whole. The opening time of praise ought to have a substantial element of celebration, celebrating what God has done. Very often we have found that a great hymn of praise will rouse the gratitude of a congregation. Conversely, it has frequently seemed a mistake to start a service with an introspective hymn of the kind which the depressive William Cowper wrote – e.g. "O for a closer walk with God." Such hymns have their place, of course, but they come more naturally as a response to God's message, rather than as an approach to worship.

We live in such a humanistically-oriented society that we seldom appreciate how its focus on human needs, problems and resources subtly erodes our vision of God. When we come together to worship God we should start with God and what he has done – not on ourselves, our failures and our needs. In any case, we see these accurately only through our vision of God. There is probably no Christian present at corporate worship who is not in some way conscious of himself as a sinful, mortal, needy human being. But that is not where we begin. We begin with God, and with gratitude that he should show such love to us, sinners that we are, that he now invites us into his eternal presence through the blood of Christ.[41]

It will not be long before the sheer majesty of God and the immensity of his grace will humble us into reverence, awe and confession – but gratitude fires acceptable worship.

4 Acceptable worship is controlled by reverence and awe (Heb. 12:28 and 29)

Jesus's own words, in his awesome prayer to God just before he died on the Cross, epitomise these control-

ling dynamics in true worship: "Father . . . Holy
Father . . . O Righteous Father . . ."[42] Here he is expressing an intimate relationship which preserves both
freedom and proper fear.

It unfortunately goes almost without saying that much
modern worship seems signally to lack this reverential
awe before a holy, righteous God. The writer to the
Hebrews has reminded his readers that they have come
to "a Judge who is God of all".[43] The Greek words could
well be translated: "a God who is Judge of all". Which-
ever is the correct translation, the words remind us of the
awesome responsibility involved in true worship, and
such a reminder is timely as we rejoice in gratitude for our
freedom to worship God as forgiven sinners.

The overall perspective of these verses is of God's
judgment, with the climax in the stabbing truth that "our
God is a consuming fire."[44] The writer seems to be
deliberately harking back to the "blazing fire"[45] which
accompanied God's revelation to Moses on Mount
Sinai – an experience which was "so terrifying . . . that
Moses said, 'I tremble with fear.'"[46] God has not
changed in his awesome holiness, affirms the writer; he
remains a consuming fire. Fire burns up the dross, but
refines the gold – in our worship, as in every part of our
lives.

The two words, "reverence and awe", denote not so
much solemnity as a sense of being answerable to God for
our worship. The words should not be equated with
what is drab or dour, as though they excluded anything
exuberant, spontaneous, noisy or unrestrained. We are
being bidden in these words to take proper account of the
fact that we must answer to God for "every careless
word"[47] we utter, and that will include words used in
worship. We are all guilty of careless words when we
take part in corporate worship, whether we are liturgic-
ally orientated or not.

The beauty of silence

Reverence and awe are frequently experienced through
silence, and most evangelical Christians in particular

need to learn to worship the Lord in the beauty of holy silence. "When the Lamb opened the seventh seal, there was silence in heaven, for about half an hour"[48] – if worship is the life of heaven, then silence is an essential part of its praise. We need to be awed into silence by the presence of the Lord in our midst.

The priority of silent stillness has been written into creation itself from the beginning. In Genesis we read that "on the seventh day God finished his work which he had done, and he rested on the seventh day from all his work which he had done. So God blessed the seventh day and hallowed it, because on it God rested from all his work which he had done in creation."[49] Helmut Thielicke, the German preacher-theologian, comments evocatively on the significance for human beings (the crown of the creation) of the Creator's rest-after-work:

> Heaven and earth and all its hosts are now complete. And as the young world in all its dewy freshness exults in the surge of life . . . the Creator withdraws into a solemn, celebrative stillness. The Creator stands above all this restlessness of life and enters into the celebration of stillness . . . There is a great silence, the resting hush of the Creator.[50]

This perspective may well hold the clue to our frequent sense of rush in Western worship. We are so set on seeing time as productive of work and (inevitably) money, that we find it very difficult genuinely to rest and be still. We have failed to find God's rhythm of work and rest. We flout the sabbath principle of one full day's proper rest in seven. We flout it at our peril, because (in Thielicke's words) "the sanctity of the sabbath is built into the very structure of the universe."[51]

Not only do we need as individuals to write stillness into our daily routine; we must also reinforce such daily moments of quiet calm with a weekly pattern of quiet worship in our corporate life as the people of God. "The Lord is in his holy temple; let all the earth keep silence before him."[52] Then, like God himself, we will be continuously refreshed, instead of driving ourselves to a standstill; "in six days the Lord made heaven and earth, and on the seventh day he rested, and was refreshed."[53] He is a proud and foolish man who thinks he can outwork his Creator – and that without due rest. Is this not the profound significance of the "sabbath rest"[54] available to God's people?

Most people who are responsible for leading worship actually find even a brief silence rather threatening. We think we have lost control, or that everyone has "switched off" or stopped concentrating. We are anxious lest something way-out is slipped in and we will not know how to cope with it. Worse still, the others will think we have lost control or dozed off! Silence thus often produces embarrassment instead of expectancy. It is important, therefore, to teach the importance and the value of silence.

There have been times when I have been present for ten minutes or more of absolute silence in a congregation of several hundred. They have been times of intense divine presence, when the love and the beauty of Jesus have been virtually tangible. These times have broken impenitent hearts, rekindled faded enthusiasm, brought clarity in confusion, and ministered peace and hope to the distraught. In addition, in such times of silence God is able to speak with distinctive precision and power through specific gifts of the Spirit.

It could well be that such distinctive communication from God to his people remains in short supply in many local churches, simply because we provide scarcely no opportunity through silence for these particular gifts to operate. It is, after all, in the corporate worship of the Church that they are intended to flourish for the common good. When this is inhibited through lack of expectant silence, such gifts either lie dormant and unused, or they are pursued in private groups of like-minded people with no proper counterbalance in other gifts, or (most dangerous of all) they become expressed in one-to-one ministry as definite (and definitive) "words from the Lord" with

no arena for evaluation and discernment of true from
false.

Where the worship of a congregation is touching
eternity because it is directed towards God, fired by
gratitude, and controlled by proper reverence and awe,
there God will speak into the silence as his people wait
expectantly for him to minister to them.

5 Acceptable worship is the fruit of consistent living (Heb. 13:15)

So far we have concentrated on the worshipping life of
God's people gathered together. It would be both naïve
and dangerous, however, to think that we can somehow
drum up acceptable worship on Sunday amongst people
whose lives do not demonstrate the presence of God
from Monday to Saturday. This is clearly indicated in
these words: "Through him (Jesus) then let us continually offer up a sacrifice of praise to God, that is, the fruit of
lips that acknowledge his Name."[55] Acceptable worship
is a gift and it comes "through Jesus". It is either a life
style ("continually" literally is "through everything") or
it is non-existent.

This is underlined by the fact that such worship is "the
fruit of lips that acknowledge his Name". Lips that
acknowledge the Name of Jesus hold the key to acceptable worship. Sadly, confessing Jesus as Lord (because
"Lord" is the Name which is above every other name,[56]
the Name which enshrined total authority and full divin-
ity) has been virtually reduced to "giving your testimony" in a church building or religious meeting. When
the New Testament talks of bearing testimony and ack-
nowledging the Name of the Lord, it is thinking of the
market-place, the godless, totally pagan scene of daily
living. Unless those who crowd a church building on the
Lord's Day are engaged in that kind of daily testimony,
where it really counts, there can be no acceptable
worship. That kind of worship is "the fruit" of acknow-
ledging Jesus as Lord before the world – i.e. the natural

outgrowth of a consistent life of daily witness to the Kingship of Jesus.

Present your bodies

Paul put it like this: "I appeal to you therefore, brethren, by the mercies of God, to present your bodies as a living sacrifice, holy and acceptable to God, which is your spiritual worship."[57] When the local church gathers on a Sunday out of that kind of daily living, it will be absorbed by the gift of acceptable worship as a demonstration of God's presence in the midst. Nothing less can do the trick – neither splendid hymns, nor a full building, nor a persuasive leader, nor singing in tongues, nor inspirational preaching.

In other words, acceptable worship involves our total being, our whole lives. It means presenting our bodies to God, with every created faculty available to him for his control and glory. The psalmist understood this when he sang: "My soul longs, yea, faints for the courts of the Lord; my heart and flesh sing for joy to the living God."[58]

If we are to present our *bodies* to God as essential to this acceptable worship in our daily lives, there is surely no reason why this should be suspended on Sundays. For historical and sociological reasons, not for any good biblical ones, we have allowed dance and drama, colour and variety to be squeezed out of the worshipping community. We have virtually surrendered the arts to unbelievers, and our worshipping life is impoverished. This is doubly tragic in the light of what previous generations of worshipping Christians have bequeathed to the world and to the Church in painting, sculpture, poetry, drama, music of all kinds.

In the West we also have a fear of total worship. The mind remains in strict control, and we are frightened of what the Bible calls our "guts". Worship which includes, and even emanates from, our guts is by no means inferior. For Jesus himself his ministry over the total range of human need sprang from his guts, according to the Gospel records.[59]

There are six occasions in the public ministry of Jesus when, in the words of the Authorised Version, "he was moved with compassion." When we examine these, we discover that they cover the whole range of human need. The Greek word at the root of this expression is *splagchna*, which means literally "the bowels or guts" of a person. The Hebrew mind saw the guts as the seat of our emotions. Jesus was deeply moved in his guts when faced with the spiritual emptiness and harassment of the crowds: they were "like sheep without a shepherd". Later we read of his compassion for the sick, and for the hungry. Mark records Jesus's compassion for a leper, Luke for the widow of Nain's son. His response to this spectrum of human need matched its variety: he sent out missionaries to bring the good news of God's kingdom to the spiritually lost; he taught those hungering for God's word; he healed the sick, cleansed the leper, fed the hungry and raised the dead.

In these comprehensive ways Jesus presented his body to God as a daily, living sacrifice. This was his life of worship, and he brought the needs which affected and moved him deep in his guts into his prayer life. Followers of Jesus today, as in every generation, are called to a similar ministry and to the same compassion. That means we will find ourselves deeply moved by the compassion of Jesus, moved to active goodness and moved to total worship with every fibre of our being. As God brings us into wholeness, integrating our daily experience with our regular worship, so we will make what we feel as much as what we believe a part of our worshipping life.

Thus, gratitude and reverent awe will touch and spring forth from our guts. Many of us are too sophisticated by far in our picking-and-choosing what we will accept in our worship. Our own sophistication often prevents worship which is acceptable to God. It certainly closes us off from innumerable Christians who, in their ready response to gut-level motivation, find conventional worship stifling.

6 Acceptable worship is a sacrifice (Heb. 13:15)

This single word, "sacrifice", lays bare all our personal tastes and whims in worship. If acceptable worship means daily presenting our bodies to God as "a living sacrifice", then the specific activity of corporate worship is also "a sacrifice of praise". A sacrifice is costly; it requires the same attitude as expressed by David when he declared: "I will not offer burnt offerings to the Lord my God which cost me nothing."[60]

This hits at our hearts when we come to a service of worship to get, not to give. We have all fallen into the trap of criticising this or that part of the service because it did nothing for us. Our approach to worship was not to bring our whole being to God and give him everything. We wanted to be blessed, uplifted, built up, challenged, instructed. We came, in other words, as children of our age – wanting our own needs met, our desires fulfilled, our problems solved. The essence of offering up a sacrifice of praise is that we deliberately say "No" to ourselves and "Yes" to God. We take our eyes off ourselves and fix them on him. We forget about ourselves, concentrate on him and worship him. That is a sacrifice because we may not feel like it or want to do it. It is a matter of "losing ourselves" in God.

In nitty-gritty terms, this will mean saying "No" to our personal tastes. It is not coincidental that the most common barrier to true renewal in a local church is the choice of music. We cannot, for example, afford to be dominated by the organ. It is a magnificent instrument and needs to be allowed full scope in worship. But there are many other instruments which need to be brought into play. In most congregations there are several people with musical gifts who would love the opportunity of playing or singing to the glory of God in an orchestra of some kind. When we began this in Cape Town, several cherished ideas – about personal tastes and the need for quality above all else – had to be subordinated to God's priorities for worship, i.e. in Spirit and in truth. Any attitude which sees performance as the purpose of such musical contributions risks the displeasure of God. Certainly we give the very best we can, but we must not be so naïve as to pretend that such a principle cannot easily be turned into an exclusive and self-glorifying exercise.

Musicians in the front line

Though not synonymous with worship, music is probably the single most important tool for worship. It is predictable, therefore, that the music will be the number one target for enemy action in a church which means business with God. Those responsible for the music are in the front line of the spiritual battle. If they can be lured into putting their own tastes, pride and reputations in front of God's glory, Satan has established a crucial bridgehead in the life of that church.

Over and over again local churches have had to recognise the reality of this spiritual battle. Sometimes organists, choir-masters and directors of music have either been sacked or compelled to resign. Less confrontive leaders have just allowed the situation to continue until either an unsuitable person has felt it right to leave or has been so transformed by the Holy Spirit that a whole new attitude prevails. There cannot be acceptable worship so long as such a situation is not resolved. And, if there is no acceptable worship in a church, virtually everything else is substantially stymied.

We have often found – both in Cape Town and in Oxford – that harmony and vitality on the musical side of the Church are the determinative factors for the healthy growth of the whole Christian community. Jehoshaphat discovered this secret when pressurised by enemies from Moab and Ammon. After prayer and seeking the Lord with fasting, "he appointed those who were to sing to the Lord and praise him in holy array, as they went before the army, and say, 'Give thanks to the Lord, for his steadfast love endures for ever.' And when they began to sing and praise, the Lord set an ambush against the men of Ammon, Moab, and Mount Seir . . . so that they were routed."[61]

If the stakes are as high as this when it comes to the worship of God's people, we cannot afford any "prima donna" attitudes to take root in the Christian community, particularly amongst those with responsibility for leading worship. Personal preference and individual taste must be subordinated to the higher dictates of God's glory and purposes. When anyone in the Christian community insists on his own way, there is invariably some hidden agenda which needs to be uncovered and thrashed out. That is simply another way of saying that worship is a way of life, and that Sunday worship reflects the daily lives of each participant – more pervasively and seriously if those leading the worship have unresolved conflicts and tensions.

We can, by this stage, begin to appreciate why the life of a local church depends on the quality of its worship. A Christian community worth the name will show its distinctiveness pre-eminently through its worshipping life. Because everything else stems from worship that is acceptable to God, it is surely worthwhile laying the whole matter before the Lord as a congregation with an open-ended prayer: "Lord, you are looking for those who will worship you in Spirit and in truth. We want to be such worshippers. We cannot make ourselves like that. Please work in us to produce a worshipping people, and show us what we need to do to make a straight path for your feet."

2 Love of the Brethren

"Let brotherly love continue."[1]

In the distinctively fragmented society of South Africa, we reached the stage in our parish in Cape Town in 1975 when some fresh initiatives in breaking down interpersonal barriers were desperately necessary. Whatever else the life of the parish was achieving, there was no obvious breakthrough in personal relationships between Christians of different colours.

When we looked more closely at these relationships we noticed that colour was not, in fact, the most pervasive factor for such distancing from one another. Those of the same racial background and with similar interests, cultural influences and education also related to one another very superficially. We had, in effect, never learned to love one another with the love of Jesus.

This was a painful, if not surprising, discovery. If the new commandment given by Jesus means anything – "Love one another, even as I have loved you"[2] – it is establishing the primary truth that such love alone will demonstrate to "all men" that we really are his disciples.[3] I remember wrestling with this challenge over several weeks of long leave from Cape Town in 1975. How could we encourage one another to move forward into something more Christian and more satisfying, as well as more relevant to the clamant needs of the society where God had placed us?

The way ahead became apparent in that particularly clear way which, from time to time, provides us with an unmistakable word from God. He seemed to be saying plainly: "Come together *for worship*: come once a month; come to celebrate the eucharist; come in an informal atmosphere – and I will draw you together across all the barriers and boundaries to love one another." A month or so later, we began "Parish Praise" on this basis, and it became a key focus for growing understanding, accept- ance and concern. As we discovered new dimensions of worship, we began to discover one another as brothers and sisters in the family of God.

That simple, but basic, discovery was particularly im- portant in Cape Town where the obscenities of apartheid legislation have produced some extremely ugly and traumatic situations in many families. About twenty-five years ago, the racial classification "Cape Coloured" was introduced as another legal grouping alongside blacks, whites and Indians. Those placed within this category trace their ancestry to (from the mid-seventeenth century onwards) the European merchants, settlers and sailors, who miscegenated with indigenous Hottentots and Bushmen in the Cape. These original natives of this southernmost area of Africa were brown-skinned rather than black. Their descendants today look everything from very dark-skinned to very fair.

When the classification "Cape Coloured" was formal- ised in the mid-1950s, the Nationalist government used three criteria to determine who should have this classi- fication: the first two were straightforward – those who looked Cape Coloured, and those who habitually mixed with Cape Coloured people. That left a sizeable minority who could not be classified. So the authorities told such people that they themselves could choose, either to opt into white privilege or to identify with the majority of their companions and families as second-class citizens.

In our large multiracial parish we had several families where this frightening decision had led to agonising disruption: one child decided to "become white", while another (born to the same parents) stayed with the rest of his relatives who had no such option. As can readily be imagined, that led to deep bitterness, with sons and daughters being completely cut off and ostracised for choosing to associate with the privileged élite rather than their own kith and kin.

The need for reconciliation

I have taken time to explain the situation in Cape Town because such deep-seated hatred and alienation (however uniquely caused by the cancer of apartheid) is common to most communities. Jesus is concerned to drain out the pus from such broken relationships in the Christian community. He does this as, by his Spirit, he applies to us the reconciling power of his Cross. As we are brought to our knees before him there, we find peace with God and then the power to relate as equals (equally responsible for sin and equally receivers of forgiveness) to those from whom we have been separated, or at least distanced, for years.

This is what we were privileged to see beginning to happen in that local church in Cape Town as we met together around the Cross as brothers and sisters in God's family. The power of true worship to produce such mutual love is unique. Festo Kivengere, Bishop in Uganda, once remarked that "evangelism is the overspill of fellowship"; perhaps we need to take the process one stage further back and say that "fellowship is the overspill of worship."

It is easy to pull to pieces modern, particularly Western, expressions of fellowship. It is far more creative to see what Jesus meant when he taught, and expected, Christians to love one another as he has loved us.

When he gave the first disciples this new commandment, Jesus was speaking in a specific context – in the upper room on the night before his death. There were eleven men present in that room. Judas had already left to conclude his appointed business. In prefacing his account of these events and Jesus's final words to his followers, John writes: "Having loved his own who were in the world, he loved them to the end."[4] He then describes the footwashing, the final appeal of love to

Judas, and (implicitly) the institution of the Lord's Supper. Then Jesus says: "Love one another like this."[5]

I have become increasingly struck by the crucial importance of John 13, especially of chapters 13–17, for appreciating the meaning of true Christian fellowship and what love of the brethren must include. This is clearer when we recollect that in these five remarkable chapters John has recorded the nub of Jesus's last words to his close friends in that final, dramatic and poignant night before his death. In action, teaching and prayer he spells out what it means to be his disciples – in the intimate atmosphere of an upper room with his twelve closest colleagues and friends. The proper application of these chapters, therefore, is not in vague generalities about the worldwide Church, but in the fellowship of a few Christians whom God has called to share in his life and love. This is likely to be in the commitment of a smaller home-cell in which the realities of being the Church of Jesus Christ can be explored and expressed.

The implications of such love for one another become clearer as we look more closely at John 13. Six aspects of Christlike love for one another stand out in that chapter: the secret of giving, the necessity of service, the possibility of misunderstanding, the absence of options, the reality of rejection and the menace of individualism.

1   Love and the secret of giving (John 13:1–3)

Jesus was able to give, and to carry on giving, himself to his disciples – and to everyone. There seemed no end to his capacity to love. The twelve disciples were in a unique position both to verify this infinite capacity to give and to point out inconsistencies or failure. They never did so. In fact, John (who was closest to him for those three years) specifically comments: "Having loved his own who were in the world, he loved them to the end."

What was the secret of his giving? How can we learn to love one another like that? The answer is laid out for us in John 13:3: Jesus knew that "the Father had given all things into his hands, and that he had come from God and was going to God." His life was based on three certainties: his relationship with God, where he came from and where he was going. With these three cornerstones in place, Jesus was free to give himself away to others. He did not need to prove anything, either in terms of his relationship with God or to assure himself of his identity and purpose in life. He was secure in the unconditional love of God, whom he knew as an all-wise and all-compassionate Father. He did not need to justify himself before God or man, either friend or foe. He was a person with a clear mission, living under authority and therefore possessing authority in his words and actions.

Above all, Jesus knew where he was going. He had one goal, and he pursued it vigorously and single-mindedly. That goal kept him moving forwards in the darkest moments and when he felt entirely alone in the world. He quietly rested in the assurance that God had "given all things into his hands" (John 3:35), even the keys of death and hell, "power over all flesh" (John 17:2). He put this conviction with total simplicity at the end of this pregnant evening, when he declared unambiguously: "I came from the Father and have come into the world; again, I am leaving the world and going to the Father" (John 16:28). That was the fundamental conviction of Jesus as the Son of God.

The heart of the Christian Gospel assures all believers that we enjoy precisely the same assurance. We have been made sons and daughters of the living God "by adoption and grace". We are heirs to all the Father's resources and he has given all things into our hands – "all things are yours . . . the world or life or death or the present or the future, all are yours."[6] Our lavish Father says – and goes on saying – to us: "All that is mine is yours."[7] Our relationship to him is as secure as that enjoyed by Jesus. We do not have to prove anything to him, let alone justify ourselves.

Frequently it proves true that real love fails to flow in a local church because Christians do not enjoy that security. The results of such uncertainty are many: for example, there are those who cannot give themselves to others because it is too painful; they feel that they will be diminished or that the cost will be intolerable; they fear rejection or that they will not be appreciated. Others find it as difficult to be on the receiving end of love because they feel they do not deserve it, or because they see the love as artificial or manipulative (e.g., what is he after?). Such attitudes to giving and receiving love from one another are often transferred either to or from our relationship with God. In particular, the feeling that we must earn love dies very hard.

If, by contrast, we know that we belong to God, that we have been given access to the grace of God in Jesus, that God chose us in him from before the foundation of the world, that we have been appointed by him to live for his praise and glory and sent to bear fruit for him by practical love and goodness of all kinds – then we are free to give ourselves to others without fear in the power of the Holy Spirit. Jesus told these disciples that the bottom line of such effective Christian living is the realisation that "apart from me you can do nothing" (John 15:5). It is very clear that we cannot by ourselves love one another as Jesus has loved us. Without him we can achieve nothing in this – or in any other – direction.

If, then, we feel hopeless non-starters in this matter of love for one another, we are in a good position provided we immediately reaffirm who we are in Christ, where we have come from and where we are going.

2   Love and the necessity of service (John 13:4–5)

There is a breathtaking humility in the action to which Jesus was moved by his complete self-assurance in the love of his Father. From our worldly perspective, we expect the experience of inner strength so vividly described by John in v. 3 to lead to some impressive display of power. On the contrary, Jesus stoops to wash his disciples' feet. There is significance, surely, in every detail of this loving service, as Jesus divests himself even of his ordinary, everyday garments and girds himself with a towel.

It would be tempting to stress here the need for love to be demonstrated in specific action. Love is a matter of deeds, not words. But that statement, true as it is, does not lay bare the essence of Jesus's love in washing the disciples' feet. That, surely, lies in his willing adoption of a servant's place before them. Love serves one another. That certainly means action, but many actions are mere gestures or public performances, not loving service.

Jesus recognised that his calling was to be a servant. He did not do the odd servant-deed; he offered himself to others to serve them. His love showed itself by this servant-attitude. There was nothing servile in this, because he invested servanthood with dignity and sacrifice. He demonstrated his greatness in serving others.

This perspective is very important in the life of a local church, where its activities and ministry can easily become a platform for people's talents instead of a fellowship in which by love we serve one another. The overall witness of a church in its local community can also degenerate into being exclusive or triumphalist. The result of such attitudes is that the Church does not from within kneel to serve the community but stands outside its pain and sin – often, indeed, against the community – in a judging spirit.

The love of Jesus frees us to ask others how we may best serve them. Indeed, his love enables us to see how we may best serve one another, and to bring that service to one another. Such love actually can discern a person's needs more accurately than he can perceive them himself. We have probably all been struck from time to time by the sensitive love of a friend who has discerned our need before we mentioned it or even recognised it. That is a reflection of the servant-heart.

It has become increasingly and painfully clear to me in recent years that I can easily see the life of the Church as providing me with the opportunity to exercise my gifts and to find personal fulfilment. If I am prevented for whatever reason from thus expressing myself freely, I become impatient and crotchety. I can now see that I have signally failed to demonstrate the spirit of servanthood, which involves looking for opportunities to attend to the needs of my fellow Christians, rather than scope for my gifts. We have only to look again at the example of Jesus to realise how unchristian such an approach is.

Because love is essentially seen in serving one another and thus making myself available to others in their needs, it stands to reason that the biggest obstacle to such loving service is any spirit of rivalry or competitiveness in a church. Love fundamentally rejoices in the gifts and blessings of others, seeks to promote and release them. The competitive spirit is the antithesis of such love and reveals a deep insecurity about our acceptance by God, even our acceptability to God. Such competitiveness easily spoils, and ultimately can control, relationships in the Christian community. It can creep in between vicars and curates, colleagues in ministry, one church and another, different groups within a church, the leaders of one organisation and the leaders of another in the same fellowship.

It seems to be a particular temptation when we are expected, for whatever reason, to exercise some authority in the Church. The ordinary pattern in worldly scenes is easily repeated amongst believers, as we forget that the contrast in Jesus's teaching between secular authority and Christian authority is complete – "it shall not be so among you; but whoever would be great among you must be your servant, and whoever would be first among you must be your slave; even as the Son of man came not to be served but to serve, and to give his life as a ransom for many."[8] On this basis we can expect to become more and more released in servanthood as we grow in the likeness of Jesus.

3 Love and the risk of misunderstanding (John 13:4–5)

Because love in action on the Jesus model is so unfamiliar anywhere else but in the Church (and rare here as well), there is bound to be a lot of misunderstanding when it is clearly demonstrated. Jesus himself found this in the upper room. Peter was probably only expressing the thoughts in each one of the disciples' hearts: "Lord, do you wash my feet?"[9] Jesus was content to leave till later any thorough explanation of what he was doing, and why he was doing it. No doubt the full implications of washing their feet remain unclear to us also.

At this point in Peter's discipleship he had revealed little understanding of loving servanthood, however often Jesus had talked about it and demonstrated it in action. Peter also found it difficult to be on the receiving end of humble service: he was a strong, self-resourceful, independent man and he did not appreciate or relish being made to accept service from Jesus – particularly when Jesus made it plain that such receiving was indispensable to discipleship. In addition, Peter certainly had little or no concept of the nature of being washed, cleansed, justified and sanctified: that became gloriously clear after the death and resurrection of Jesus and in the gift of his Spirit.

For all these reasons – and probably for others – Jesus met with complete misunderstanding when he washed the feet of his disciples. Such misunderstanding occurs today when people see love in action in true servanthood. There is certainly misunderstanding in the minds of unbelievers. For example, the servant-love of those who choose for Jesus's sake to lay down their lives (or certainly their prospects and their careers) in serving the poor at home or overseas is often misconstrued by, and usually remains a mystery to, the outsider.

Parents, in particular, find the decisions of their Christian children about their vocations extremely hard to appreciate or understand. Within the Church it is sadly true that those who opt out of endless meetings in order to bring Christ's love to people in need of all kinds are often regarded with suspicion and misunderstanding. Those who lay down their lives in serving others in humble caring are held in admiration; but sometimes this admiration seems tinged with a slightly sceptical attitude, reflected in almost patronising concern: "Isn't she doing too much and going a bit far in helping others all the time?"

I think, if I am honest, that I have this attitude at times to my wife's steady commitment to serving others in the love of Jesus. She is constantly, if not continuously, giving herself to others out of unselfish sensitivity to their needs. She has learned to be a servant in a way I have not begun to experience. I think I fail to understand or appreciate this spirit of servanthood. I sometimes resent it, because it gets in the way of my peace and comfort. I know it is my self-centredness which makes me rebel against her Christlikeness. I sometimes choose to interpret her desire to serve others as a reflection on my inadequacies instead of rejoicing in the love of God shed abroad in our life together as a family through her example.

If I can misunderstand and resent the love of Jesus lived out by my wife, then I will surely fail to appreciate its worth and priority in the fellowship of the local church. I am no different as a husband from what I am as a member of the Church. The same self-centredness operates in the Church fellowship as at home. And I am probably no different from anyone else in the Church. So there will always be the risk of misunderstanding when the servant-love of Jesus is made evident in the Church. The closer we are to one another, the more misunderstanding will occur. One clear example comes in the way the "willing workhorses" in the Church are presumed on for endless tasks – because they seem to be readily available, their presence and efforts are taken for granted and their feelings often ignored. When, on the other hand, such loving servanthood is joyfully given and recognised, then there is a release of mutual support and then individual Christians find true fulfilment.

4 Love and the absence of options (John 13:12–20)

Instinctively we all hope there might be some other way than the costly path of love. Jesus makes it plain that there are no alternatives. First, he has set us an example in the servanthood of his own life. Secondly, if we rightly call him Lord, we have no option but to obey him when he commands us to follow his example. Thirdly, we will never find true happiness except in obedience to his clear commands. Fourthly, our attitude to our brothers and sisters in Christ reveals our attitude to Christ himself, who comes to us in our fellow Christians. There is no way round these four perspectives on the priority, the unique claims, of love.

This challenge comes home to roost in the life of our local church. Jesus is unequivocal in asserting that "he who receives any one whom I send receives me."[10] Yet we find it very difficult to accept one another as sent by the Lord to be our brothers and sisters. There is an inordinate amount of church-swapping today. Even within the same church it is not uncommon to find Christians opting out of one home-group to join another. Why? Because they don't get on particularly well with one or two people.

This selective approach to Christian fellowship is one of the most destructive forces in today's Church. It is clear from the Gospels that the twelve disciples did not exactly hit it off together all the time, and it is very likely that Jesus was addressing this fact in his statement in John 13:20 – because they were often at odds with one another, and they very probably resented the presence of particular individuals in the group of twelve. When we think we can exercise one of several options in choosing our Christian brothers and sisters, we betray a number of misapprehensions. The most serious of these is the assumption that fellowship is a matter of basic compatibility, similar interests and backgrounds, and personal preference. In other words, we reduce fellowship to a pleasant mixture of purely human qualities in a Christian atmosphere.

The New Testament, by contrast, consistently portrays fellowship as supernatural in origin and essence. It cannot be produced by human beings at all. It is the gift of God's Spirit and transcends all natural characteristics. It is fundamentally sharing in Christ together, seeing Christ in one another, and being enriched by knowing God's grace through one another. Christians do not automatically discover fellowship by being together. The corollary of this truth is that Christians actually discover true fellowship in the Holy Spirit when they do *not* have anything else in common except their experience of God's salvation.

When, therefore, we find we do not get on very well with other Christians, that is precisely not the time to opt out into a more congenial fellowship. On the contrary, at that point we are on the brink of discovering what true fellowship in Christ is all about – *if* in faith we look for Christ to manifest himself in those whom he has given us in that local church or home-group or whatever.

If there is one current tendency which threatens to undermine God's work of revival in his Church today, it is this immature separatism which so readily distances itself from Christians who think, act, sing, pray, talk or dress differently from our own personal tastes. This trend is another example of the self-indulgent humanism which has so pervaded the Church in the twentieth century: if I like it, I will; if I don't, I won't.

Jesus presents us with no such options. We are called to love all those who call on his name in the place where we live. The small home-group where he has placed us now is a good arena to begin to work out this commitment.

5 *Love and the reality of rejection (John 13:21–30)*

Three times already in this chapter reference has been made, directly or indirectly, to Judas. In John 13:2 the writer notes that "the devil had already put it into the heart of Judas . . . to betray him." The Lord himself has indicated his own awareness of the presence of a traitor in John 13:10: "You are clean, but not every one of you." In 13:18 he refers more explicitly to an imminent fulfil-ment of a powerful prophecy in the Psalms: "He who ate my bread has lifted his heel against me."[11]

The shadow of Judas's greed and treachery looms large over the intimacy of these personal conversations. Jesus had looked forward with intense longing to sharing this

Passover-meal with his close friends. [12] No wonder he
finds himself deeply "troubled in spirit" (John 13:21) as
the reality of Judas's betrayal presses its clammy hand on
the atmosphere. He had loved Judas as much as anyone
else. Time and again in the previous three years there had
been opportunities for Judas to turn back from the way of
treachery. Even at this last hour Jesus gave him a distinctive sign of his love, in offering him the morsel of bread
dipped in wine – the mark of special friendship.

Both Jesus and Judas knew this was the final chance for
the betrayer to draw back from his chosen path. John
crystallises the moment of awesome truth with the
words: "Then after the morsel, Satan entered into him"
(John 13:27). Until that moment Judas was still in a
position to resist the insinuations of the devil. From then
on he was a pawn in the devil's hands. Jesus knew this
and told him directly: "What you are going to do, do
quickly."

Judas chose to reject the love of God. The important
point about his rejection, in terms of the love we are
called upon to show as Christians, is that God's love in
Jesus is not irresistible. Individuals can – and some do –
choose to reject Jesus and his love. What this brings
upon them is frightening: what it does to Jesus himself
we can only guess; but, if our own experience of seeing
our love rejected is anything to go by, it must produce in
our Lord the most agonising suffering.

Whenever we allow the love of Jesus to control and
sustain our relationships, we run the very real risk of
rejection. No doubt the career and the fate of Judas were
unique; nevertheless, there are still many occasions
when men still find it too costly to receive the love of God
through another person – and therefore push it aside in
order to press on in their own resources and along their
own planned road.

It is very painful to stand back and watch people
rejecting the love of God. It happens all the time in
pastoral ministry and in evangelism. Often it looks as
though people deliberately choose to turn their backs on
the love of God when it is plain to all (including them-

selves) that this is the only way forward. They inflict
increased pain and suffering on themselves and on many
others by their rejection of God's love. There are few
situations in which we taste our helplessness more acute-
ly, and it is important to remind ourselves that Jesus has
experienced such rejection and that he never insisted on
ministering to those who were not ready for his love.

There is a very important note of realism in Jesus's
acknowledgment of Judas's position. It is noticeable that
the new commandment – "love one another even as I
have loved you" (John 13:34) – is given only after Judas
has left the house. If Judas had been unable to respond to
the love of Jesus in his own soul, he was in absolutely no
position to receive and respond to this command. That
still holds good: it is impossible to love another person
with the love of Jesus unless we have opened up
ourselves to his love. The new commandment becomes a
millstone around the necks of any who have refused to let
the love of Jesus deal with their own fears, ambitions,
resentments and pride.

6 Love and the menace of individualism (John 13:36–38)

Peter once more takes the centre of the stage. This time
his defences are completely down, and we see him in all
his lovable, but dangerous, independence. Jesus has
painstakingly unfolded the very heart of his longing for
his disciples. There has been no ambiguity about his will.
Indeed, he has couched it in terms of a commandment –
completely new and utterly revolutionary. If, as seems
obvious, Peter was under many illusions about some
facets of Jesus and his kingdom, the one reality he never
doubted or questioned was the love of Jesus for him,
Peter, and for all the disciples. Peter could not, therefore,
have missed the dynamic thrust of that new commandment – and yet he did.

Instead of quietly allowing its impact to sink into his
impetuous heart, he latched on to something Jesus had
declared he could not do. Now Peter never liked to admit
that there were certain things – any *one* thing – which he

could not do. He was already jibbing at Jesus's words.
His pride was rising up in protest. So Jesus, in his love for
Peter, has to reiterate what he has just said: "Where I am
going you cannot follow me now." Earlier (John 13:33) he
had said this to them all; in 13:36 this is in the second-
person singular, as if to press home the point to Peter that
he is not a special case. The commandment to love one
another, and thus to demonstrate to the world ("all
men" – verse 35) that they are his disciples, applies to
Peter as much as to the rest.

Peter did not think the new commandment sufficiently
important to distract him from his own personal glory-
trip for Jesus: "I will lay down my life for you" (John
13:37). Peter saw his own martyrdom as more significant
than obedience to the new commandment. That is the
menace of individualism. God's Church today suffers
from the driving ambitions of those who reject the implications of the new commandment. This is particularly
true in the life of a local church. I have often agonised
about what more to do for those who persist in keeping
their distance from the local fellowship because they
have their own agenda for personal discipleship.

Sometimes, I freely admit, such distancing is understandable. Certain Christians feel that if once they allow
themselves to be caught up in the treadmill of Church
activities their authentic witness in an unbelieving world
will be eaten up in religious meetings. Such fears, if well
grounded, need to be examined and their causes removed.

More frequently, the individualism of such Christians
stops them identifying with the local family of God in any
realistic or costly way. If they are linked with other
Christians in genuine fellowship, it is entirely with
people of their own choosing, not with those whom
Jesus has sent to them.

The net result is an overall shallow obedience to the
new commandment throughout the local church. An
attitude grows which sees other things as more important, in spite of the clear teaching of Jesus. It is most
important to see individualism for what it is, especially its

modern manifestation in Western society, notably the
United States. It is another example of the tentacles of
humanism – not simply that man is the measure of all
things, but that ultimately this one man (I myself) matters more than anyone else or all others.

We properly affirm our individuality in freedom of
thought, speech and action – but we then proceed to do
our own thing in isolation from one another, and God's
precious gift of individuality becomes perverted into
individualism. We then fail to discover the glorious Gos-
pel-truth that we find our selfhood, our personhood, our
individuality only as we lose it. Jesus calls us to lose it for
his sake in his body, the Church. We discover our individuality, in fact, in total commitment to one another in
the body of Christ.

Paul actually puts this truth with the utmost succinct-
ness and simplicity in two parallel passages: "As in one
body we have many members, and all the members do
not have the same function, so we, though many, are one
body in Christ, and individually members one of
another."[13] The other passage is equally plain: "You are
the body of Christ and individually members of it."[14]

The message is clear: we find our individuality, not by
standing at a distance from one another but by carefully
nurturing our relationship with one another as members
of one body. To return to Peter and the menace of his
individualism: at the very moment (with the imminent
departure of Jesus) when the togetherness of the disciples was absolutely fundamental, he wanted to do his
own thing. Time and time again this fatal flaw has
weakened the life of the Church at the critical point when
immense strides could have been taken to deepen and
extend the fellowship of the Holy Spirit.

The key phrase for implementing such obedience to
the new commandment is mutual submission. This is
particularly necessary for all those in leadership in a local
church. It would be good for such people to ask themselves this question: am I prepared to put my ministry
and leadership on the line and let the body of Christ here
decide what is best, both for me and for the Church as a

whole? By and large, all of us in such positions find that exceedingly difficult to do.

On at least two occasions in the past I ought to have done this – and did not do so. On one occasion I had the courage to let others in the local church assess the rightness/wrongness of a possible move. The contrast between those two situations and this latter one was most marked in terms of impact on the quality of fellowship in the church. My individualism made obedience to the new commandment more difficult, indeed burdensome. My submission to my fellow Christians revealed the freedom and the joy in that same commandment.

Peter thought the only valid way to lay down his life was to do so physically and literally. Although Jesus actually did that in his love for us, he had been laying down his life from the moment he left the glory of heaven and continuously throughout his time on earth. He wanted his disciples in their inner being to accept a life of mutual love of the same kind – laying down their lives for one another in everyday, nitty-gritty ways.[15] Such sacrifice, such daily saying "No" to ourselves and "Yes" to one another, is perhaps more difficult than actual martyrdom. It is not at all glamorous. It does not pander to our pride. It will often go unnoticed and unheralded. For all these reasons it is not the way we would naturally choose. Only the love of Jesus himself for us can bring such a motivation, and go on bringing it day in, day out in our life together as Christians in our local church.

Laying down our lives

If, therefore, the new commandment means anything, it means being prepared actually to lay down our lives for one another. As a Christian husband, I can appreciate (and feel profoundly humbled and convicted by) the force of Paul's instruction to me to love my wife in that way, to lay down my life for her in the way that Christ loved his bride, the Church.[16] But I find it very difficult indeed to conceive of the possibility of laying down my life for people I do not really know. I see them across the

aisle on a Sunday morning. I know the names of a few. I
meet with them and many others on several Church
occasions. But I do not really know them at all. I am
ignorant of their real needs and longings, their joys and
sorrows. And they are equally ignorant of mine. And this
situation will persist so long as the life of a local church is
made up of services and meetings of this kind.

Jesus gave the new commandment to eleven men who
had spent the best part of three years living in one
another's pockets. They had slept and wept, walked and
talked, agreed and argued – *together*. There was hardly
anything that they did not know about one another. They
were of different temperaments and backgrounds. They
were divided in their political leanings and loyalties.
What is most important is that they had spent these three
years in the company of Jesus. They had seen his love for
them. They knew the meaning of love in action. When
Jesus told them to love one another as he had loved them,
they were under no illusion as to what it meant (at least in
theory).

The first decades of the Christian Church confirmed
the reality of such love in the community of Jesus's
disciples. By the end of the first century, pagans were
saying in genuine amazement: "See how these Christians love one another." Paul was able regularly to give
thanks to God for the love which flowed in different
churches. There were a few which lacked it (notably
Corinth), but he could write: "It is my prayer that your
love may abound more and more."[17] Or again: "We
always thank God . . . when we pray for you, because we
have heard of your faith in Christ Jesus and of the love
which you have for all the saints."[18] Or again: "We give
thanks to God always for you all . . . remembering . . .
your . . . labour of love."[19]

If such love for one another was such a striking feature
of local churches then, it must clearly be possible now.
But one thing is sure: neither in the first nor in the
twentieth century did this love grow under human com-
pulsion. We cannot make Christians love one another. I
suppose there is no church anywhere in which members

do not want more Christlike love to fill the fellowship. This kind of love is a gift because "the love of God is shed abroad in our hearts by the Holy Spirit."[20] In other words, any efforts to fill the local church by beating one another about the head and urging us to greater love are bound to be abortive. Love for the brethren, like acceptable worship, is a gift from God to his Church, the fruit of his Spirit at work in the Christian community. That, presumably, is why the writer of the letter to the Hebrews says (13:1): "Let brotherly love *continue*" – it lies latent but actual in the body of Christ: let it continue to grow. The most difficult aspect of loving one another is keeping it up.

Most Christians have probably experienced, at some time or another, a demonstration of Christ's love through the selfless concern of another person. We have, therefore, a clue about what is possible. The thrust of the new commandment is more direct and thorough: we are instructed to love one another like that all the time; we are also given no choice about those whom we are to love like that. In other words, every member of the local church is to be receiving and giving this love day in, day out. That is the way Jesus loved his disciples. No doubt some of them were more lovable than others. No doubt even Jesus had moments when he might cheerfully have dropped them all into the Dead Sea from a big height. But he loved them all to the end.

Meeting one another

When we look for reasons why such love, however fleetingly present in certain places, is generally so absent from local churches today, we are inevitably drawn back to the whole question of structures – both the structures with which we seem to be lumbered, and the structures which we generally do not possess. Most churches have innumerable meetings of different kinds in order to carry on the business. But how many of these meetings actually enable people to meet God and to meet one another? Do Christians have as a priority a regular commitment to

meeting with a few others in order to grow into this
Jesus-love?

Normally, Christians are so busy with meetings of
different kinds that there is no time left to build good
relationships of the kind Jesus nurtured with his disciples
and then enjoined on them just before his death. Such
quality relationships must surely be at the top of our
agenda. At this point we do well to remember that the
early Church did not have large, impersonal buildings set
aside for sacred things. They met in one another's
homes, regularly in the same homes. The New Testament often speaks of "the Church in your house". These
home-churches could not have contained large numbers
of people. It is difficult to be precise, but the minimum
would probably have been fifteen to twenty and the
maximum fifty to sixty.

If there is one single priority for local churches in these,
or any, days, it is to establish a network of such home-
churches, in which Christians can learn to love one
another with the commitment and self-respect of Jesus
Christ.[21] Where this has happened in recent years, a
significant breakthrough has occurred. At the same time
as we introduced "Parish Praise" in Cape Town, as
described earlier in this chapter, we were establishing
several home-churches. This combination of central
celebration and intimate fellowship became the matrix of
immeasurably improved relationships – both towards
God and one another.

Over five years later, when we were in Oxford, we
were visited by a family of six who were spending a year
away from Cape Town in York. The father, a very able
and self-resourceful man of about forty, had been one of
the first to join (and host) a home-church in 1975. He had
been a most reluctant participant at the outset. He had
many friends, a pleasant and powerful personality, a
successful career, a delightful family, a lively and relevant faith. Deep down he felt he did not need the closer
commitment of a home-church. He was quite happy to
join a group for Bible study, but not so sure about
exposing himself more fully.

When we asked him what he missed most about Cape Town, he unhesitatingly replied: "Our home-church." Over five years they had become so committed to one another in love, that the separation was like a mini-bereavement. Through being linked at this depth to many different Christians in his area he had in fact encountered the kind of people he would never have chosen as his friends in the normal course of events. In that home-church, for example, there was an ex-prisoner who was divorced from his wife and needed regular, sacrificial support in order to maintain him in his Christian discipleship.

Growing pains

In such microcosms of the Church, which can genuinely begin to model the pattern set by Jesus with his disciples, love for the brethren begins to grow. The process will always be accompanied by growing pains. Without proper commitment to one another (even with it) it is tempting to give up when things get difficult. If, however, we are to be obedient to the new commandment and if we are to follow the injunction to let such love continue, we must encourage one another to persevere.

The consistent witness of the New Testament indicates that this quality of love is not optional. John makes it plain that the supreme evidence of a person's having been born again – and thereby having become a child of God – is precisely the fact that he loves "the brethren" with the love of Jesus.[22] If then, such love is obligatory, not optional, we are bound to make ourselves vulnerable to its demands and implications. That will mean opening ourselves up to one another so that the love of God can begin to control and direct our life together. When this happens, such freedom to share both what we are and what we have will steadily grow. The fellowship of the early Church included sharing of possessions and property.[23] It is, of course, possible to share possessions without ever sharing ourselves. In most Western countries today members of a local church find it difficult to share either themselves or their possessions. The remarkable statement of Luke about the Jerusalem Church – "No one said that any of the things which he possessed was his own"[24] – pinpoints the inbuilt possessiveness of most Christians. The transition from "me and mine" to "us and ours" is long and arduous. And love is nothing if it is not practical.

This kind of life style will inevitably involve a radical re-examination of our weekly schedules and an excising of any number of meetings and organisations which may well be useful and good in themselves but which make effective involvement in a home-church impossible. The life of a true home-church demands commitment in time and loyalty.

It is necessary to point out more explicitly the world of difference between home-churches and such common activities as prayer-groups, Bible-study groups or other home-meetings for fellowship or evangelism. The home-church is what it says, the Church in the home. Everything, therefore, which from the New Testament we expect of the Church, we expect to develop gradually in the life of a home-church. It will include Bible study, prayer, evangelism and many other ingredients, but it will not be restricted to any one or two. Above all, the emphasis will be on loving one another, i.e. on the quality of personal relationships.

Here it must be said that, in many existing Bible-study groups, the one thing which seems, by mutual consent, to be excluded is any depth in relating to one another as people. Often it is the case that Bible study is used as an excuse to avoid such honest relationships. The text of the Scripture is used to reinforce the barriers behind which people hide from one another.

Round and round the roundabout

We will never, of course, arrive as a local church at the place where we are truly loving one another with the love of Jesus. This is inherent in the nature of the love of God, "which surpasses knowledge",[25] and therefore can never be plumbed, attained or exhausted. On a visit to Cape Town in 1976, Colin Urquhart described the round-about which any alive church inevitably reaches. It goes round and round, apparently not progressing any further. There are a number of roads off the roundabout, marked with various signposts like "more evangelism", "the healing ministry", "deliverance of the demonised", "social involvement". The Church tries one or two of these broad roads, but they all lead back to the roundabout. Finally, someone notices a little dirt-track marked "Love one another" and tells us that this is the way to go. We are convinced that we already love one another and that there must be some other route to our destination. But God brings us back to that little dirt-track and he says once more: "Love one another."

If the leadership of a local church is not ready to open up in this way, it is extremely unlikely, if not impossible, that the Church as a whole will be able to travel this road. Most ministers and pastors are lonely men, often forced into that loneliness by the expectations of their people, the professionalisation of the ordained ministry, and the driving need to succeed – or at least not to fail. Many shibboleths have been drummed into them, one of which is the danger of having close friends in your own church. I was myself taught this by men of worldly wisdom but of severely restricted freedom in personal relationships. It has taken a long time to unlearn it, and I still find it difficult to appreciate what the Bible really teaches about the nature of true friendship.

Each year we as a staff go away for three or four days, in order to review the past year, be refreshed in the Lord, enjoy being together and look ahead to the coming year. I remember well one relaxed evening on one of these annual retreats, when we decided to spend an entire evening open-endedly affirming one another by saying what we appreciated in each person. I suppose there were about a dozen in the room. We began at eight and finished well after midnight. I am sure that different people had different experiences that evening, both in expressing personal appreciation of colleagues and in having their own strengths and gifts underwritten.

My overriding memory is of the impact on my self-awareness of hearing those close to me and working with me point out what they appreciated in me as a person. I remember very little of what they said, but I do remember being made painfully, but creatively, aware of my faults, weaknesses, failures and sins. As my friends affirmed me, I had the freedom to see my negative side and my no-go areas. They never mentioned these – by mutual agreement we all concentrated on the positive. Instead of being on the defensive because my weaknesses were coming under the microscope, I was made more keenly aware of these as I heard and felt this positive acceptance and appreciation. Indeed, I am sure that I expostulated at some stage: "But can't you see this and that which are all *wrong*?"

Now I think I am aware of the need to speak the plain truth, uncomfortably and in love, when the occasion demands. But the analytical, cautious, evaluative mind of most English Christians often leaves little or no room for positive, unalloyed appreciation. True friendship in Jesus and the truthful love of Jesus are often best expressed without the "if only" and the "yes but" of the careful critic. I have a suspicion that many ministers and pastors in this country would blossom, both in ability and in approachability, if they heard rather more appreciation.

For many years I looked on the story of David and Jonathan[26] with some wistfulness because it enshrined an experience of friendship which seemed elusive. By temperament I am, like many others, more shy than extrovert. By inclination I prefer many acquaintances, with whom I get on well, to a few really good friends who will not be afraid to put me in my place. I sense that the most profound reason for my preference for superficiality is because I want to run my own life and do not relish my freedom being infringed. I have an in-built, but mostly undefined, fear of letting others get too close.

Gradually these natural tendencies are being eaten

away, mainly because a few close friends have insisted, in love, on drawing alongside and speaking the truth. This has not always, or even usually, been in any sense confrontive. In fact, most of the time they have sensed my need of support, encouragement and affirmation. They have underlined the significance and the strength of true friendship. These few people I know I can approach with my real self, my greatest needs, temptations, desires and weaknesses. They will not be shocked or censorious. I trust they would feel the same freedom for themselves with me.

The quality of friendship enjoyed by David and Jonathan is eminently possible in the love of Jesus Christ. It is, I believe, what he envisages as the life-blood of the Christian community. It is his intention, not just for a few individuals for a brief while, but for each person all the time. Such love is God's gift by his Spirit to each local church. "Let brotherly love continue."[27]

3 Love for strangers

"Do not neglect to show hospitality to strangers, for thereby some have entertained angels unawares."[1]

It is unpleasant being a stranger. I remember standing on one of the main streets in the centre of Buenos Aires in 1976. I was on my own. I could not speak the language. I had never been to Latin America before. I knew nobody and nobody knew me. I felt – and was – a complete stranger. I felt extremely vulnerable and exposed. I could have disappeared without trace, and nobody in Argentina would have been any the wiser.

The New Testament sees people without God as strangers – Christless, stateless, friendless, hopeless, Godless.[2] When you know you do not belong, you can be lonely in a crowd. If we are cut off from God, we do not belong in his family. However much love there is flowing in a local church, the stranger will still feel an outsider – but that same love is to be lavished on the stranger. There is only one way for strangers to become citizens – through the reconciling death of Jesus on the Cross. It is the privilege and task of the Christian community to demonstrate God's reconciling love in action at the Cross by its welcoming love to all such strangers.

The Greek word translated "love of the brethren" at the beginning of Hebrews 13 is *philadelphia*. In the second verse the writer uses a word from a similar root, *philoxenia*, which means literally "love for strangers" but has come to mean "hospitality" – presumably because we can best show practical love to strangers by opening our homes to them. But the main effect of moving from *philadelphia* to *philoxenia* is to ensure that we do not as

Christians allow ourselves to get inward-looking in our love for one another, but move outwards all the time to those who are strangers to God and his Gospel.

This love, as with *philadelphia*, will be uninhibited and unrestricted. It will involve sharing ourselves, our homes, our time, our possessions, our Lord. It is both costly and comprehensive. A family in Oxford got to know another family when one member was in hospital. They spent hours together, worked through many crises; they gave time, cash, discipline, and always acceptance. But there was one thing else they brought – the Gospel. In the end it was the Gospel that brought change. Help which does not include telling the good news is like trying to block up holes in a colander one by one. True love for strangers will include evangelism, as we take time to get to know and relate to the whole person.

Open homes

The Greeks' instinct for seeing hospitality as the essence of love for strangers is still accurate. Opening up our homes remains the most effective and the most appropriate way to show Christ's love to strangers. We need to introduce a word of warning at this stage: we are not to open up our homes to outsiders in order to convert them, but because we love them and want to share ourselves with them. The challenge has been put this way: do we love people in order to win them to Christ, or do we win people to Christ because we love them?

Hospitality is a mutual experience. If we open up our homes out of love to those who are strangers to the love of God in Christ, we will find that they will do the same to us. And it is precisely at this stage in the proceedings that, once again, our structures and our schedules cause an almost intolerable strain. Why? Because "keen" Christians are so caught up in church meetings that it is often difficult to find any spare time. That fact in itself betrays a false sense of values, for which those in leadership of local churches must carry most of the responsibility. We have allowed a philosophy to arise –

and at times we push it ourselves for all it is worth –
which measures love for Christ in terms of attendance at
meetings.

Yet the malaise often goes even deeper. It has reached
the point where many Christians in fact do not have
genuine friendships with outsiders. Their social life is
spent almost exclusively within the activities and community of the Church. A contributory reason for this
"holy huddle" syndrome is a false understanding of
worldliness. A certain kind of Christian has come to see
"the world" as "out there" – wicked places, doubtful
behaviour, unbelieving people. John pins us all down
here because he makes it plain that the world is inside us
all – "what the sinful self desires, what people see and
want, and everything in this world that people are so
proud of".[3]

Every Christian is called to live distinctively *in* the
world, and that means having as friends those who do
not know Christ. It is salutary to take a look at our diaries
and to see how often in the last few months we have
spent an evening, let alone a day, with outsiders. One
of the revealing truths about sharing the Gospel with
strangers is that the most effective Christians are those
recently converted to Christ – because they have not
been eased out of their friendships with non-Christians.

The over-churchiness of our lives as Christians probably explains the relative ineffectiveness of so many
evangelistic ventures, such as guest-services, missions,
door-to-door visitation – even supper-parties. Strangers
to God's love have an inbuilt suspicion of such special
efforts, particularly if they come at them like a bolt from
the blue without a context of caring, open-ended
friendship.

We have, sadly, inherited approaches, even attitudes,
to evangelism which bypass loving people. Jesus loved
men and women into following him. Any evangelistic
efforts without love are useless. Paul calls them "a noisy
gong or a clanging cymbal".[4] If we realised that outsiders
often see our evangelistic methods and activities in this
way, we would call a halt now to most of them. Paul's

own verdict on loveless evangelism is: "I am nothing . . .
I gain nothing."[5]

An evangelistic life style

Love will, of course, find many creative and imaginative
ways to come alongside those who are strangers to God.
The love of Christ controlling a local church will drive its
members out all the time in sustained evangelism. The
New Testament sees such evangelism as a way of life,
with every Christian under an obligation to share the
good news in every way possible.[6] The Acts of the
Apostles gives countless examples of this evangelistic life
style. Like the accounts in the Gospels of the ministry of
Jesus, the Acts lays considerable stress on the use of
homes for such daily testimony. It will hopefully whet
our appetites to take a further look at the pivotal place of
the home in any ministry of love for strangers.

The Middle-Eastern emphasis on the importance of
hospitality is well known. Jesus clearly played the local
culture and customs throughout his ministry. There
seem to have been three major arenas for his activity –
the synagogue, the open air and different homes. These
were the major meeting-places of his contemporaries: so
he spent his time there. The first two places will have
local distinctives in each generation and culture, but
homes remain the same.

In Luke's Gospel this emphasis is plain. A brief panor-
amic reading is very revealing, beginning with his healing Simon Peter's mother-in-law of a raging fever in
Simon's house. By the evening of that same day the home
had become the target of every sick person in the
neighbourhood.[7] Such ordinary and straightforward
ministry (Simon's mother-in-law probably had the
equivalent of the 'flu) would today turn Christian houses
into a focus for healing and wholeness in the local community.

The next chapter has two striking incidents in homes.
In the first, Jesus is pressing ahead with his teaching
ministry. In the middle of it, "the power of the Lord was

with him to heal" (an important insight into the active authority to bring results which Jesus demonstrated in his teaching), and a paralysed man is brought to him on a stretcher by four friends. Let down through the roof because of the crush inside the house, the man receives both the assurance of forgiveness and the healing of his paralysis.[8] So this Galilean home became the scene for the Lord to display the fullness of the Gospel.

Throwing a party

This is immediately followed by Levi's (or Matthew's) conversion from the dubious occupation of tax-collecting. What did he do? "Levi made him (Jesus) a great feast in his house; and there was a large company of tax-collectors and others sitting at table with them." Jesus issues a clarion-call to repentance at the dinner-table, as well as using the carping criticism of local religious bigots to talk in joyful terms of celebration as the heart of his message.[9]

Jesus was invited on several occasions into the homes of Pharisees, his most bitter critics and opponents. Luke records three separate occasions when Jesus accepted such invitations, using them to share his good news with the guests – often in a very direct manner. On the first occasion he reprimands his host for failing to treat him with the normal courtesies dictated by current conventions, and then proceeds again to his central theme of forgiveness.[10]

On the second occasion he goes straight to the heart of the matter, almost before they all sit down to the meal. When the Pharisee expressed astonishment to see Jesus not washing his hands before dinner, Jesus in effect replies, "Make sure you wash your heart – it is filthy, full of violence and evil."[11]

On the third occasion, a Sabbath-day, Jesus deliberately heals a man whose legs and arms were severely swollen, and then gives very pithy instructions about giving feasts for the poor and needy, rather than the usual tit-for-tat party-giving indulged in by the well-to-do. He finishes off the evening with a devastating parable emphasising God's eternal concern for the needy, to the extent of issuing his invitation to such people to sit down to dinner in the Kingdom of God because the more privileged (like the Pharisees) considered such an invitation unimportant.[12]

These three examples provide us with a strong incentive to make time for accepting similar invitations and, once present, to be utterly fearless and direct in declaring the truth of the Gospel. The instructions of Jesus to the Gadarene demoniac, now "clothed and in his right mind", come to us with equal relevance: "Return to your home and declare how much God has done for you."[13] Such personal testimony, at parties in our own homes and when invited to the homes of others, is of the essence of sharing ourselves with strangers and outsiders.

Luke's Gospel provides several other cameos of Jesus at work in homes – for example, raising Jairus's daughter from the dead; ministering to the distracted Martha in the Bethany home so beloved of Jesus; and assuring Zacchaeus of salvation in his wealthy house in Jericho.[14] Children, housewives, wealthy businessmen – Jesus loved them all, ministering to them in the privacy and familiar security of their own homes. It is reasonable to assume that all these homes became centres of healing, teaching and ministry of all kinds. Capernaum, Bethany, Jericho: a fishing town, a quiet village, a bustling commercial centre – all knew the transforming touch of Jesus, as individuals, families and homes became like beacons in the local community.

In the light of Jesus's own pattern of ministry, his instructions to his twelve disciples, and later to the seventy sent out in pairs, become particularly significant. To the twelve he gave "power and authority over all demons and to cure diseases, and he sent them out to preach the Kingdom of God and to heal."[15] His specific orders included the following: "Whatever house you enter, stay there and from there depart."[16] Similarly, when he commissioned the seventy, he explained: "Whatever house you enter, first say, 'Peace to this house.' And if a son of peace is there, your peace shall rest upon him; but if not, it shall return to you. And remain in the same house, eating and drinking what they provide, for the labourer deserves his wages; do not go from house to house. Whenever you enter a town and they receive you, eat what is set before you; heal the sick in it and say to them, 'The Kingdom of God has come near to you.' "[17]

Homes as bridgeheads

After allowing for the distinctives of these two commissions and for the specifics of that particular culture, we can still see the importance of an evangelistic, teaching and healing ministry carried on persistently and sensitively in a local community. The Church in that place is sent by the Lord to penetrate the homes and the meeting-points of the community. This is what happened in the Acts of the Apostles, as the first Christians shared themselves in loving compassion with their neighbours. This is encapsulated in these words: "Every day in the temple and at home they did not cease teaching and preaching Jesus as the Christ."[18] Peter's ministry at Joppa, a seaside town on the Mediterranean coast, was based at the home of Simon, a tanner. From there he was moved by God to Caesarea to the home of Cornelius. In both Joppa and Caesarea Luke tells us that Peter stayed in each home for many days.[19]

Paul's ministry follows a similar pattern. At Salamis in Cyprus, his first evangelistic initiative after being sent out with Barnabas from Antioch, he is summoned to the house of the Roman proconsul, Sergius Paulus. There Paul's teaching, together with an astonishing demonstration of God's power upon Elymas, the proconsul's resident magician, brings the Roman official to faith 'in Christ.[20] At Philippi the home of Lydia became Paul's base of operations. Later on, the home of the chief jailor at Philippi Prison witnessed a joyful household-baptism.[21] At Thessalonica Jason's home acted as headquarters for Paul and Silas's ministry, and their host had some extremely awkward moments as a result.[22] At

Corinth Paul first met up with a well-to-do couple, Aquila and Priscilla, whose home became his own home, and the meeting-place for a home-church, both in Corinth and later in Ephesus.[23] When Paul had shot his bolt in the synagogue at Corinth, his ministry continued next door in the home of Titius Justus.

In Ephesus some remarkable happenings took place in one particular home where Paul was clearly carrying on a very effective ministry amongst those with evil spirits. One such person was approached in the house by some seven itinerant Jewish exorcists, who presumed to use the name of the Lord Jesus as a magic incantation. All seven were sent scattering, "so that they fled out of the house naked and wounded".[24] Obviously we need to expect some unusual happenings if we open up our homes in this way, not least in damage to furnishings and equipment.

Perhaps the most concise account of Paul's ministry in homes comes in his own description of his work at Ephesus, where he lived for nearly three years – the longest time he spent in any one place. Of this period he declares: "I did not shrink from declaring to you anything that was profitable, and teaching you in public and from house to house, testifying both to Jews and to Greeks of repentance to God and of faith in our Lord Jesus Christ."[25]

This résumé of God's ministry through Jesus, Peter and Paul (as recorded by Luke) has been given to reinforce my plea that local-church evangelism should be concentrated on Christian homes, and that Christian families should see hospitality, given and received, as the main method of expressing the love of God to those who are at present strangers and outsiders. In the extended family context of a home-church, such opportunities to express love for strangers can become fuel for frequent intercession. The whole home-church will be concerned for such families and individuals. This will provide a vital cutting-edge to the life of the home-church, as well as making it possible for all its members to work together in providing hospitality in this way.

Cutting out meetings

With many local churches organised as they are, this might well mean a number of active Christians opting out of meetings and organisations specifically in order to release time for such strategic opportunities. If this does happen, such people would need to communicate their decision, and the reasons for it, to their minister. Speaking personally, I would love to have my timetable pruned of innumerable church meetings so that we could open our home more frequently and purposefully to our neighbours. After over four years in Oxford, we feel that we have hardly begun as a family to share ourselves and to share Christ with those around us.

It is important to add one more factor in exposing the way Christians so often fail to show the love of Christ to strangers. In a word, we are afraid of people without Christ. We have a fear that we will be out of our depth, that we will have nothing in common, that our neighbours will discover all the holes in our discipleship and our faith. It is good to take these fears out from under the wrappers which rationalise them, and to admit that, in essence, they reveal nothing but selfishness and lack of love for those without Christ. We are concerned more for our reputations and security than for their salvation and eternal destiny. Fear is always like that, and this is why it is Satan's major weapon. Through fear we are turned in on ourselves; through love we forget ourselves and go out to others.

If we are aware of being gripped by such fear, we need to bring it directly to God, who wants to cast out all fear through his perfect love for us,[26] and to fill us afresh with that love which he has for the whole unbelieving world[27] – and particularly for the friends and neighbours down the street. Love for strangers, like love for the brethren and acceptable worship, is God's gift to his Church. Nothing can shake it because it is of the essence of the Kingdom of God.

4 Love for the under-privileged

"Remember those who are in prison, as though in prison with them; and those who are ill-treated, since you are also in the body."[1]

There are, of course, strangers and strangers. Anyone who does not know Jesus Christ is a stranger to God's love, and God wants him to become his own child. But there are certain strangers who, if the emphasis of Jesus's own earthly ministry is a reliable guide, are to come particularly within the reach of our love. In the verse above, the writer to the Hebrews refers to "those who are in prison" and "those who are ill-treated".

The imprisoned and ill-treated were the special concern of Jesus. He came to seek and to save those in the prison of some physical or moral bondage – the prostitutes, the demonised, the blind, the lame, the paralysed, the leper. He sought out those whom the system or the authorities or the culture of the day treated with less than justice and compassion – the social outcasts, the have-nots, those rejected because of their race, the poor, those hated because of their background or their chosen way of life.

Each local church is called to an authentic imitation of Jesus in its life style. John puts it like this: "We may be sure that we know him (i.e. Jesus), if we keep his commandments. He who says 'I know him' but disobeys his commandments is a liar, and the truth is not in him; but whoever keeps his word, in him truly love for God is perfected. By this we may be sure that we are in him: he who says he abides in him ought to walk in the same way in which he walked."[2]

If we are to walk in the same way as Jesus walked, we need to look more closely at his walk. Again, the Gospel of Luke provides us with as penetrating an insight as any. The first instance is "a man full of leprosy".[3] The social, religious and psychological implications of this ugly disease are underlined later in Luke's Gospel when ten lepers met Jesus on the outskirts of a village somewhere between Samaria and Galilee.[4] Apparently, lepers were social outcasts and had to live outside the community in a special compound. They were not allowed inside the village or town and, if anyone came near to them, they had to ring a bell in warning.

The book of Leviticus devotes two whole chapters to the theme of leprosy.[5] Elaborate investigation was enjoined on the priest, acting on behalf of the whole community, to establish whether an individual had in fact caught the dreaded disease. Once confirmed "the leper . . . shall wear torn clothes and let the hair of his head hang loose, and he shall cover his upper lip and cry, 'Unclean, Unclean.'. He shall remain unclean as long as he has the disease; he is unclean; he shall dwell alone in a habitation outside the camp."[6] There were also elaborate precautions carried out by the priest to establish that a person had been healed of the disease, and that is why Jesus, on both recounted occasions, told the healed lepers to go straight to the priest for a check-up. Only the local priest could actually readmit a healed leper to the social and religious life of the community.

The socially ostracised

Leprosy hardly occurs in most countries in the world today. On the other hand, there are a number of conditions which lead to similar ostracism. They vary in different kinds of society, but they are to be no less a target for the local church's love for strangers. For example, in spite of social welfare rightly made available in many countries, the elderly and the handicapped are usually pushed to the margins of the community. Not only will the Church of Jesus Christ initiate special programmes for senior citizens and those who are either mentally or physically handicapped, it will also encourage its members not to adopt the attitude so often prevalent in society at large, especially in the family life of Christian homes. The Church will particularly stand up for those who are, of all people, unable to speak for themselves – i.e. unborn children and the senile. These are fast becoming the most vulnerable of all those marginalised by modern social norms.

It is, of course, easy to be naïve about the emotional and physical cost of family care of this kind. This is where the shared concern of an "extended" family through the life of a home-church comes into its own. It is much more realistic to think of fifteen or so people with different ages, backgrounds and family responsibilities pooling their resources to care for such marginalised people.

Luke's next portrait of Jesus at work with social rejects is that of the tax-collectors.[7] They clearly intrigued the doctor-evangelist. He gives the impression that they flocked to Jesus, probably because Jesus was virtually the only person to take the initiative to befriend them. Tax-collectors were not popular in Roman-occupied Palestine. 'Pukka' Jews reckoned they had sold their soul to the enemy by agreeing to work for the invader. Added to this treachery, they were notorious for exacting more than was required and pocketing the excess. They were a wealthy élite, whose chosen careers and ill-gotten gains made them friendless and lonely. We can imagine them locked up behind their well-guarded walls in the most attractive part of town, longing for someone to break through their self-imposed prison bars.

The up-and-outs

Jesus unerringly went for their Achilles heel, their love of money. With Levi it was an uncompromising "Follow me"; with Zacchaeus it was inviting himself to a meal. Jesus faced these "up-and-outs" with himself as their friend – but entirely on his own terms. He knew they were as much in prison as those condemned by the Roman authorities for insurrection. It is significant that Jesus's parables about a lost sheep, a lost coin and a lost son were addressed to a company which included tax-collectors as well as those whom the Gospels regularly called "sinners", who in the main were prostitutes and pimps.[8] These strangers needed the love of God in a special way.

In most communities today we can find the modern equivalent of the tax-collector. He also will live in a comfortable part of town. He will keep very much to himself, because he has little option. His business reputation will not be very high. His marriage will be on the rocks, and his children will be alienated from him and from people in general. He will have inside a desperate longing for someone who is not interested in his money, but in him as a person created in the image of God.

It is not surprising that tax-collectors and prostitutes resorted together to Jesus. They would, in any case, have been not unfamiliar to one another. What is striking is the ease with which Jesus "walked" amongst these women of the city. Not for him the aloof coldness which emphasises distance, not compassion. Particularly impressive is his behaviour towards the woman in Simon's house, who "began to wet his feet with her tears, and wiped them with the hair of her head, and kissed his feet, and anointed them with the ointment".[9]

Christians have not usually found it easy to follow the example of Jesus in mixing with those of lax morals in sexual matters. We still tend to react with a special revulsion when faced with the kind of situation in which Jesus was so manifestly free and clean. No doubt we have attitudes and desires which need to be brought to the Cross for cleansing and for redirection by the Spirit. When a local church can move freely and creatively in the area of sexuality, it will find countless opportunities for sharing the love of God with many men and women whose lives are in a mess because they have confused love with sexual gratification.

This is specifically needed with the increase of practising homosexuality. The compassionate love of Jesus longs to set men and women free from the bondage which these practices seem uniquely to produce. There will scarcely be one local church where this kind of ministry is not needed. Christians who have discovered the liberating power of Jesus by his Spirit in these areas are the best ministers of God's love to those still imprisoned by past events and present relationships.

The racial issue

One of the most bitter feuds in Jewish society in the time of Jesus was a racial one – "Jews have no dealings with Samaritans."[10] Several times we read of Jesus deliberately rejecting the inbred racialism of his contemporaries. He faced it directly when it reared its ugly head amongst the twelve disciples. James and John, not for nothing nicknamed "Sons of thunder", were furious when the inhabitants of a Samaritan village refused to have anything to do with Jesus. "Lord," they expostulated, "do you want us to bid fire come down from heaven and consume them?" Jesus's reaction was uncompromising: "He turned and rebuked them, saying, 'You do not know what manner of spirit you are of; for the Son of man came not to destroy men's lives, but to save them.' "[11] He was clearly indicating that vindictive racialism is satanic in origin. There are certainly few aspects of human behaviour more obscene.

There can be little doubt that the story of the good Samaritan,[12] which reads far more like an actual event than a strict parable, was told by Jesus to stress that our neighbour is anyone in need whom God brings across our path, and that social (and other) conventions are there to be ignored. Jesus himself broke through all these barriers which caused men to be so bitterly divided, and he calls his Church locally to express this breakthrough. In many communities nowadays there is a substantial number of immigrants. So far from keeping our distance from such strangers in our midst, let alone joining any bandwagon which wants them to be repatriated, the Christian community has a special opportunity to share the love of God with them.

Although that sharing can never, in integrity with the teaching of the New Testament, compromise the uniqueness of Jesus (his work, his message and his identity), we must still take sensitive time to understand the culture and beliefs of people from another background altogether. Jesus's own method with the woman of Samaria near Sychar is a classic: showing the utmost sensitivity, he was utterly uncompromising in directing her away from the focus of her inherited religion – Mount Gerazim – to himself as the source of living water, as the Messiah.

If Jesus directed his ministry both to the perpetrators and the victims of racialism, he also cut across the attitude which had grown up in Jewish society towards beggars. The Old Testament had very clearly and consistently enjoined upon the Jews the priority of compassionate care for the poor. This obligation had been fended off and rationalised over the years, and beggars were treated with much the same embarrassment and disdain as today. By contrast Jesus made a particular point of ministering to such people. In fact, he had to overcome the attempts of his own disciples outside Jericho to impede Bartimaeus from meeting him.[13]

I personally find myself reacting to such social pariahs in a way precisely like those disciples, and precisely not like Jesus. I suspect that I am not unusual in this. It is convenient to have the Salvation Army round the corner, and I am genuinely glad that Oxford City Council and Simon House (a work carried on by the Cyrenians) do a great deal for such folk. Indeed, within half a mile of Oxford city centre there is also a Church Army hostel and a night shelter for homeless people. But I am still clear in my mind, if not in my heart and will, that the local Christian community could do far more to find blind Bartimaeus and to minister redemptively to him. The ministry may not be immediately effective, as proved to be the case with another blind man at Bethsaida;[14] but long-term care is what the Church in a local community is equipped to provide.

Gripped by the occult

Luke, in common with the other evangelists, highlights the way Jesus set free people gripped by evil spirits. The occult practices of contemporary society had left a trail of demonised men, women and children. Luke's narrative[15] describes such symptoms as uncleanness, violence, dementia, wandering, tormenting, wildness, convulsion, shrieking, foaming at the mouth, racking pain, dumbness, moral degeneration, physical weakness, a crooked spine. There are a large number of occasions when similar or other symptoms are *not* attributed to demonic forces. Equally, Luke was a doctor and he carefully reports cases which include a demonic element, as well as many which do not.

Contrary to much modern thinking, the situation today is not very different. Television programmes broadcast particularly for children often contain such material. Scarcely a teenager passes through high school without some exposure, however brief and harmless, to some practice or other of this kind. There is, consequently, no need for any local church to start looking for people afflicted by demonic forces. They are all around us. When Jesus entered situations where such people were present, the power of the Holy Spirit within him exposed the true nature of such dark forces. When a Christian community is operating in the power of the Spirit, the same exposure will happen. Then the love of God will bring release to those thus imprisoned and ill-treated by the devil.

It would be unfair on Luke to leave this overview of his account of Jesus's ministry to those rejected or ignored by society, without concentrating for a moment on two major groups of people often mentioned in this Gospel – women and children. Neither was given much place or honour in contemporary Jewish, Greek or Roman society. One common prayer was uttered daily by many a

Jewish man: "I thank Thee, Lord, that Thou didst not make me a woman."

Jesus and women

Luke highlights Jesus's ministry to women, and also the important ministry which they had to Jesus. Not only do we have his very full account of the conception, birth and early days of both John the Baptist and Jesus[16] (in which the limelight falls fully on Elizabeth and Mary), but we also have a fascinating reference to Mary Magdalene, Joanna, Susanna "and many others, who provided for Jesus out of their means".[17] Luke records Jesus's ministry to Simon Peter's mother-in-law,[18] the widow of Nain,[19] the woman at Simon the Pharisee's house,[20] the woman in the crowd with severe haemorrhaging,[21] Mary and Martha[22] – and he particularly noticed the widow's mite.[23] Luke also notes the costly faithfulness of the women who had come with Jesus from Galilee: they stood watch by his Cross and prepared spices and ointments for his body; they were first at the tomb on Easter morning, and heralded the message of his resurrection to the apostles – to whom "these words seemed . . . an idle tale, and they did not believe them."[24]

Jesus and children

Luke's descriptions of Jesus with children are equally evocative. It is probably indicative of the doctor's interest in children that he alone describes Jesus at the age of twelve getting lost in Jerusalem for virtually two whole days until his frantic parents find him in the temple quizzing the religious experts.[25] Jairus's daughter evokes the tender, powerful compassion of Jesus;[26] the demonised son of a desperate father elicits a majestic demonstration of God's power;[27] a child in the crowd silences an argument amongst the disciples about who is the greatest;[28] babies become the best description of trusting believers;[29] the frightening responsibility of causing one such "little one" to stumble is dramatically spelt out.[30]

We know also that, when the disciples tried to drive the children away, Jesus rebuked them, saying: "Let the children come to me, and do not hinder them; for to such belongs the Kingdom of God."[31] On Palm Sunday, it was the "Hosanna" of the children, acclaiming Jesus as the Messiah, which so infuriated the Pharisees. To this Jesus replied: "Yes; have you never read, 'Out of the mouth of babes and sucklings thou hast brought perfect praise'?"[32]

Jesus loved children. He wants everyone to be like them.[33] In many countries and churches today we need to be challenged about our treatment of both women and children, and in particular widows and orphans.[34] Without taking on board the thoroughgoing "demasculinisation" of religious language now prevalent in North America, we still need to make full room for proper expression of shared ministry between men and women in leadership. We also need to remind one another that children are people too – not to be shouted down and generally ignored when adults (the ones who *really* matter) are around. The local church ought to be in the forefront in showing this unique love of Jesus to those who still struggle for proper acceptance as human beings, and who bear the brunt of pain and suffering in a deprived society.

Male chauvinism and strident feminism are equally a polarisation from God's way. For about twenty years the stress has fallen on equal opportunities for women and men, with a consequent tendency to diminish the value and significance of motherhood. Today there seems, in fact, to be an increasing need – and desire – for motherhood to be re-established as a high and holy calling. The pendulum has begun to swing back towards a proper balance between a woman's fulfilment of her gifts as a person and the special gift of motherhood.

In the case of children, exploitation, on the one hand, and letting them run everyone else's lives, on the other, are alike to be rejected. Every man, woman and child is in need of the love of God in Jesus Christ. Only in this way will strangers become friends – of God and of one another. Only within the love of God will rejection, loneliness, discrimination and prejudice be overcome.

This is the way Jesus walked. His love was the same for everyone. He had no favourites. But he displayed a preferential option for the under-privileged, the imprisoned and the ill-treated. If we are to walk as Jesus walked, we must in our churches begin to penetrate our local communities with compassion and insight. Where are people hurting? Where are they looking for release? Where are they the victims of man's inhumanity to man? How can we minister the love of God to them? How can we so act as to minimise or even remove the causes of their ill-treatment?

The Hebrews verse quoted at the beginning of the present chapter gives us the motive for such compassion: "Remember those who are in prison, as though in prison with them . . . since you also are in the body." In other words, we are to put ourselves in their shoes: if that was our situation, what would we want others to do for us and to us? The reference here to being also "in the body" is, almost certainly, not a reference to sympathy with imprisoned and ill-treated *Christians* because we are all members of the body of Christ. That would be out of character with the way the writer to the Hebrews uses such words and concepts elsewhere in his letter. Rather he is reminding us that we too are ordinary flesh-and-blood human beings; when we are in whatever way imprisoned or ill-treated, we are hurt and feel pain. This is, therefore, a summons to all Christians to outdo the caring humanist in sheer humanitarian goodness and kindness. Is our Church known in the area for *that*?

5   Christian family life

"Let marriage be held in honour among all, and let the marriage bed be undefiled; for God will judge the immoral and adulterous."[1]

One of the many fascinating aspects of visiting different countries is to notice the varied approaches to family life. In Africa, for example, the concept of the nuclear family is completely unknown. A family includes uncles and aunts, cousins of all kinds, grandparents and kindred even further "removed". The word "cousin" is also virtually absent: often the terms "brother" and "sister" are used to include cousins. When the father of children leaves home for work or study, the extended family naturally takes responsibility.

In Latin countries, both in Europe and South America, there is also a strong sense of there being one family which includes everyone closely related. Families tend to be large anyway, but brothers and sisters also remain closely in touch with one another after they have grown up and got married. The fiesta spirit is one which always includes the whole family in hours of celebration, usually right into the small hours. One baptism in Malaga involved festivities until 2 a.m. It would be unusual, to put it mildly, to find an English family celebrating little Billy's christening in such a way.

The United States seems to gear its whole culture around the children. The habit of eating out is far more widely practised than in Britain. An average American family will eat out probably twice a week. The culture is specifically geared to such family occasions, whereas in Britain it is still very difficult – and positively expensive –

to eat out as a family. Only in the last ten years or so, since pubs have begun to provide food and children's areas, has it been possible to think of going out occasionally as a family. The impression still remains that children are a nuisance, and need to be pushed away into the backroom or outside.

A visitor to the United States could, on the other hand, be pardoned for thinking that "the kids" rule in American society. There is a noticeable precociousness about children in that country which is not always charming or "cute". If on one side of the Atlantic children are expected to be seen (occasionally) but not heard (or else), on the other the needs of the children are often stridently paramount and easily indulged.

The extended family

Because the cultural conditioning of family life varies so widely in different parts of the world, it is important to discover how the distinctively *Christian* character of living together in family-community can be encouraged. It seems clear that the biblical pattern of family life, both in principle and in practical outworking, is far closer to modern examples in Africa and Latin countries than in Europe and North America. From this basic fact we can draw the firm conclusion that one of the cornerstones of Christian family life is being together and doing things together, not simply as mum, dad and the kids but as an extended family. One of the many advantages of basing local church life on a network of home-churches is that it encourages this kind of shared enjoyment in a non-exclusive atmosphere.

It is probably plain by this stage that I am advocating in this book a pattern of local church life which is so centred on home-churches that it must exclude many activities traditionally integral to congregational life. To come absolutely clean would be helpful. I reckon that a local church needs its Sunday worship together and its home-churches weekly – and virtually nothing else. If the home-churches truly begin to express what it is to be the

Church in the world, there will be no need to have a multitude of different groups and organisations to cater for different ages and tastes.

What has this to do with Christian family life? Most local churches have a plethora of different activities, each geared for a particular age-group or interest-group. There are special activities for children, teenagers, singles, young marrieds, housewives, mothers, fathers, working men, working women, divorcees, widows and widowers, and senior citizens. The practical implications of such a diverse programme are serious for Christian family life. Father is out one night, mother the next, and teenage children on a third. It is often impossible to do more than join in a few minutes of a church service *as a family*. The occasions are few and far between when the whole family, nuclear or extended, can be together as a community in Christ. In other words, whereas the Hebrews verse at the head of the present chapter urges "let marriage be held in honour among all", we actually encourage families to split up and rarely plan our Church life to honour family life.

Sunday School

The situation tends to be even more serious than at first it appears. The result of the local church's schedule not honouring the family life of its members is that essential parts of Christian home life are gradually eroded out of existence. One of the thin ends of the wedge may well be the way we have, in general, accepted Sunday School as a normal and essential priority in the local church. Not only is it a comparatively recent invention in the history of the Church; it has also come to dictate the mobilisation of adult lay ministry in the congregation. The need for teachers in the Sunday School is so pre-eminent in many local churches that considerable numbers of excellent Christian workers are involved in what is essential ministry, namely the teaching of the children. But the question is this – should they be involved in this ministry? If the pupils are the children of Christian parents, the responsibility for bringing them up in the Christian faith rests with those parents, rather than with Sunday School teachers. If they are the children of unbelieving parents, why is the evangelistic outreach not directed to the adults?

When we look at the ultimate implications of investing so heavily in Sunday Schools we detect a very critical situation. The quality of Christian family life, seen with the shutters open, is not very high. Family prayers, grace before meals, and praying with the children before they fall asleep have previously been taken as read in Christian homes – yet even this bare minimum is going by default in many Christian families.

But these three practices are only external examples of what ought to be a consistent quality of family life in which the parents (and particularly the fathers) take full responsibility for discipling, as well as simply disciplining their own children. It is my own pastoral experience – and I know it to be a strong temptation in my own home – that Christian fathers spend very little time, imagination and effort in bringing up their children "in the discipline and instruction of the Lord".[2] Mothers spend much more of all three, but frequently the parental conscience is absolved by the presence of excellent Sunday School teachers.

I hope it is not necessary to emphasise how much uniquely important work is done by such teachers, who specifically give themselves week in and week out to the care of children. Without such devoted ministry, Christian family life would be even more traumatically depleted. When parents have begun to take on the major responsibility for their own children, there will surely be a proper role for those specially gifted in such ministry to fulfil it in both a teaching and an advisory capacity. I see no reason why this could not be done through the life of the home-churches, in which the full family-situation of each child will be well known and specially appreciated.

When the quality of Christian family life declines, it differs from that of unbelievers in little more than a few religious practices, like "going to church" on Sunday

mornings. When the local church is called by God to be
an alternative community in a world where the very
validity of the family is being challenged, it is crucial that
we do all we can to ensure that marriage is "held in
honour" amongst Christians in these ways.

This priority assumes even more urgency in the face of
frequent reports of Satanist prayer meetings in different
parts of the country aimed at the break-up of Christian
marriages. If the forces of evil and darkness take Christian family life that seriously, we are playing with fire if we
ignore the basic cornerstones of family unity in Christ. A
member of our church attended a wedding reception
recently where he found himself in conversation with
another guest who was not eating any food. When asked
why not, the person replied that he was fasting. Understandably assuming that he had found another Christian,
my friend expressed his happiness at finding another
believer. The retort was sharp and timely: the other
person was a Satanist fasting for the break-up of the
marriages of key Christian leaders.

Such happenings are salutary if they reinforce our
desire and our determination to build homes where Jesus
is truly Lord and King.

Christ in the home

When Christ reigns as King in the home, everything will
be brought under his Spirit's control in the home's everyday life – settling arguments, spending money, caring
for people, making and keeping friends, attitudes to
possessions, facing up to disappointments and sadness,
coping with failure and fear, valuing beauty and goodness, challenging the priorities of the world around us,
confronting evil in every form. A Christian home is not
simply a family which goes to church on Sundays: it is a
home where Christ is real day in, day out.

To mould our family life on Christ's pattern in this way
is clearly a huge task, requiring commitment and courage
of the highest order. I know I cannot do it by myself. As
our four children grow up into teenagers, we feel not just

inadequate but utterly vulnerable. We need the support of the family of God to face up to and fulfil our responsibilities to build a home where Christ rules and where marriage is held in the highest honour. I have discovered how easy it is to become discouraged and limp in the face of contemporary pressures on the family. I value greatly solidarity with other Christians, single and married, in pressing ahead in faith to exploit the resources of God for our life together. I encourage myself by recalling that marriage and family life are God's idea, plan and gift.

Even though I need support and encouragement for building our home life on Jesus Christ, I cannot afford, however, to give in to any temptation to abrogate my responsibility for my children under God under the guise of delegating their Christian growth to Sunday School teachers. I must also resist pressure from my local church when its programmes divide, rather than unite, the family. Insofar as this takes place, the church is in fact encouraging weak, low-level and even broken marriages. When we do not hold marriage in honour, we are imperilling the purity of the marriage-bed. There are very few temptations to unfaithfulness in marriage, where Christian couples are united in their commitment day by day to the awesome responsibility of establishing Christian family life in the community. As the grace of God comes up trumps through all the ups and downs of building a Christian home, so the marriage is daily secured in the love of Jesus.

There are few things more refreshing and fulfilling than being part of a truly Christian home. I well remember my own appetite for marriage in Christ being keenly whetted by the sheer joy, fun and freedom of sharing in Christian homes in my late teens and early twenties. To give young people such a model of Christian family life is arguably the very best contribution we can make for the future, especially in a world where there are so many examples of broken marriages and broken homes, amongst Christians as well as unbelievers.

There is, also, no more powerful evangelistic weapon than a Christian home where the love of God motivates

every relationship. When we become disheartened by
our failure as Christian partners and parents it is good to
remind ourselves that others looking in are usually
struck, not by our rate of success or failure, but by the
honesty and reality with which we let Jesus be Lord in
our relationships. The presence of God is far more noticeable to those who live their lives unconscious of it than to
those for whom it is axiomatic and accepted.

There is another reason why we can be very positive
about Christian homes as bridgeheads into the local
community. The three thrusts of Jesus's love described in
the previous three chapters – love for the brethren, love
for strangers, and love for the under-privileged – all
depend largely on the presence of Christian homes as the
base for home-churches.

As Christian homes become bridgeheads into the local
community we will gradually find a more biblical balance
emerging in the life style of the local church. Members of
Christian families will begin to grow in Christ and thus to
discover their God-given ministries. Instead of the active,
committed membership being concentrated on children's evangelism, this pool of talent will be available for
a wide range of opportunities amongst adults. After all,
the biblical pattern is surely to evangelise the adults,
because then the children come along with them. It
seems perverse to say that the best way to reach the
adults is through the children – perverse because it
twists both the biblical norm and the God-given order of
relationships within the home.

Positively, therefore, the local church ought to do all it
can to encourage the family to worship, to learn, to enjoy
life, to pray, to grow up into Christ *together*. Programmes
should be organised with this priority in the front of
everyone's minds. This will mean many family activities
centrally, like pot-luck or shared suppers, parties, away-
days, picnics, barbecues, etc. It also brings us back to
home-churches, where the Christian family acts as the
focus for Christians of all ages, single and married, to
come together in Christ. The home-church is not just
another meeting. It operates seven days a week, twenty-

four hours a day. It gathers together once a week for specific purposes, but gathering is only one of many activities.

Including single people

In this context Christian families become mutually supportive, and can furthermore provide the support which is essential for those who have, or choose, to live on their own. One of the common misconceptions around today is that single and married people have little or nothing to say to each other about their respective life styles. The same lie has been foisted on us in similar divisions between young and old, male and female, rich and poor, intellectual and pragmatic, artistic and prosaic. The world puts people in watertight compartments, encourages overspecialisation, delineates the expert in this or that, emphasises the differences and the difficulties between people. Jesus Christ transcends barriers, draws a variety of folk together, enables them to relate and to grow together.

In Christ, therefore, we expect to see a rich intercourse between different people concerning every aspect of life. Single people will have very shrewd insights into the problems of married couples. A sensitive father will bring wise counsel to a lonely bachelor. Grandfathers will be steady confidants of worried teenage girls. An all-out male chauvinist will get through to an ardent feminist. Youngsters will be the joy of an elderly relative's humdrum existence. Musical Philistines will open a new window on true worship for a concert pianist. The practical illustration of a down-to-earth Christian will bring to life the articulate teaching of the university graduate.

Many secular myths will be laid to rest in the open extended life of a Christian family, particularly when it provides the heart of a home-church. When society around us is disintegrating because of the gradual erosion of family life, such a Christian presence demonstrates powerfully the unshakeable nature of the Kingdom of God. Christian family life is one of God's most priceless gifts to his Church. "The Church builds families by recognising that the Church is the family of God and the family is the Church of God . . . The Church must work to build strong homes . . . so that each home is truly a church and the Church truly is a family."[3]

We do not need to spend time and energy as Christians bewailing and berating the collapse of sexual morality in our society: "God will judge the immoral and the adulterous,"[4] and judging is neither our privilege nor our calling. We are called to honour marriage and to hallow the marriage bed. There is nothing more positive and beautiful for us to do than that.

Paul's instructions to the Christians at Thessalonica in northern Greece form a pithy conclusion to this theme: "God wants you to be holy and completely free from sexual immorality. Each of you men should know how to live with his wife or control his body in a holy and honourable way, not with a lustful desire, like the heathen who do not know God. In this matter, then, no man should do wrong to his fellow-Christian or take advantage of him. We have told you this before, and we strongly warned you that the Lord will punish those who do that. God did not call us to live in immorality, but in holiness. So then, whoever rejects this teaching is not rejecting man, but God, who gives you his Holy Spirit."[5]

6 A sharing life style

> "Keep your life free from love of money, and be
> content with what you have; for he has said, 'I will
> never fail you nor forsake you.' Hence we can confide-
> ntly say, 'The Lord is my helper, I will not be afraid;
> what can man do to me?' . . . Do not neglect to do
> good and to share what you have, for such sacrifices
> are pleasing to God."[1]

So far, in examining the priorities of God's unshakeable
Kingdom, we have noted five, each of which has to do
with our relationships – with God or with other people.
The key word has been love, love for God and for our
neighbour (in different guises, i.e. our fellow Christians,
those outside the Church, the under-privileged, and
those in our own family). The writer to the Hebrews
seems to preserve, in the above verses, this emphasis on
love, because he now urges us: "Keep your life free from
love of money." In the original Greek, the sentence is
only two terse words: "life-style no-love-of-money".

The timeless relevance of the Scriptures is powerfully
evident in this injunction, especially because the writer
accurately perceives that trusting God and loving money
are mutually exclusive and rival life styles. In urging
contentment with what we have, he immediately gives
God's promises as the grounds for contentment; "for he
has said, 'I will never fail you nor forsake you.'" He
obviously appreciates the fact that we cling on to our
possessions and covet yet more precisely because we
cannot trust God with our lives. We therefore build up
earthly, tangible securities as insurance against what
might happen. Anyone who has moved house will vouch

for the frightening way in which we gather and hoard possessions of all kinds. Indeed, it is often very difficult for some people ever to think of a move because of the upheaval involved in disturbing the nest.

Fear of change is not necessarily the reason for being attached to our possessions. There are more subtle chains which love of money fashions around us. In a Christian home which tries to be open to the needs of friends, relatives and neighbours there will always be damage, breakage and other wear and tear. We have found this a constant pressure-point in our married life, not least in the way we can easily jump on the children for carelessness with material things, whereas we take similar behaviour from countless guests in our stride. This must, in some way, build up a cryptic materialism in our children, when all the time we are seeking to write in non-materialistic priorities.

The Hebrews' verses quoted above fire a double-barrelled salvo at our love of money: "be content with what you have" and "share what you have". Neither comes naturally, especially in the harsh world of modern advertising. We are constantly bludgeoned with the demands to get more, to buy bigger and better. These cries depend entirely for their effectiveness on the dissatisfaction inherent in our lower nature. Nor is it easy to share our possessions – a fact which comes out with painful force in bringing up children to be unselfish. We all instinctively want to get, rather than to give.

Covetousness is idolatry

It is important to recognise afresh the power of acquisitiveness and selfishness because we can forget the immense strength of materialism. The Bible tends to be more unequivocal about this cancer: it calls it "covetousness", and for good measure states baldly that it is "idolatry".[2] Unless we face up to the power of covetousness, seeing it as false worship and an alternative to worshipping God, we will not be in a position to resist and overcome it. When a man gives more time and money to his new car than to God, he is an idolater. When a woman is more concerned with her wardrobe than with her inner character, she is committing idolatry.[3]

If this is a fundamental temptation for every Christian, here more than in most areas we need the realistic, truthful, compassionate support of those who know us well. In the open atmosphere of a home-church, we can properly help one another to detect, confront and reverse this inner greed. In such a context it ought to be possible to reach the point where, for example, we know what each person earns and gives away. Confronting covetousness is not, of course, a matter of simple accountancy. On the other hand, mutual accountability within the non-judgmental love of God would encourage us immensely along the joyful path of celebrating unselfishly the lavish generosity of a good God.[4]

One of the most important ways of thus assisting one another in practical discipleship is by bringing our life together under the authority of the Scriptures in this matter of material possessions. Once again, Luke's Gospel contains some very pertinent material – none more so than the much-misunderstood parable of the unjust steward.[5] The passage is particularly valuable because it ends with the withering scorn of the Pharisees when they recognise the significance of Jesus's revolutionary teaching about material possessions. Luke's little aside about the Pharisees – "who were lovers of money" – exactly echoes the injunction in the letter to the Hebrews: and the Pharisees were also very religious. There are few phenomena with more potential for corruption than the combination of religion, power and money.

It is, incidentally, important to notice the nuance in Jesus's use of the Semitic word "mammon", which refers not simply to money but to all that money can buy: he calls such mammon "unrighteous", using a phrase which indicates its essential nature. We often hear Christians asserting that money itself is not evil, only that a love of money is "the root of all evils".[6] There is a

valuable truth in this distinction; but it must not prevent
us from feeling the full weight of Jesus's unequivocal –
and repeated – reference to "unrighteous mammon".
One thing is sure: "it is easier for a camel to go through
the eye of a needle than for a rich man to enter the
Kingdom of God."[7] Jesus, at any rate, was under no
illusions about the obstacles, indeed the dangers, to faith
presented by material possessions.[8] If the most important possession in the world is entering and enjoying the
Kingdom of God, it is no wonder that Jesus regarded the
most powerful dissuasive to such true happiness as
"unrighteous".

The parable of the unjust steward provides a very good
example of a fundamental exegetical principle – i.e. we
should not examine for spiritual significance the particulars of the story, but receive the lesson(s) in discipleship
which ensue. In the text of Luke 16, the parable ends in
the middle of verse eight; the lessons are contained in the
teaching from the second part of verse eight through to
verse thirteen. These lessons – there seem to be four –
provide a balanced, but challenging, perspective on
material possessions in general.

How to use our money

The first key word is: *shrewdness*. Jesus contrasts Christians and non-Christians in their basic approach to material things: "The people of this world are much more
shrewd in handling their affairs than the people who
belong to the light."[9] There is nothing at all Christian in
mismanaging our business affairs or in failing to get the
best value for money. Time and again financial experts
have just cause to be horrified at the way local churches
and individual Christians handle money. We are concerned here for wise, even shrewd, administration of
plant, possessions and capital for the sake of the Kingdom of God. Many local churches would be well advised
to review their whole administrative and financial pro-
cedure. Most clergy are not trained or competent in this

area and would be mightily relieved to see it in the hands of others more skilled.

The second principle in Luke 16 is: *strategy*. "I tell you, make friends for yourselves by means of unrighteous mammon, so that when it fails they may receive you into the eternal habitations."[10] This opens up an exciting vista of the strategic use of our money for eternal purposes. Jesus urges us to look at our material possessions from the perspective of heaven: how can I use my home, my car, my money with maximum effectiveness? God wants us to know the joy of being welcomed into our eternal home by those who turn out to be there because we gave them hospitality, or offered them a lift, or sent a regular contribution to a missionary society. There is a great sense of fulfilment in working out before God, particularly along with other Christians close to us, such strategic investment of our material resources.

The third perspective is: *scrupulousness*. Jesus's teaching here comes home very pungently. "He who is faithful in a very little is faithful also in much; and he who is dishonest in a very little is dishonest also in much. If then you have not been faithful in the unrighteous mammon, who will entrust to you the true riches? And if you have not been faithful in that which is another's, who will give you that which is your own?"[11] These words turn our accepted values upside-down. Jesus sees material possessions as not belonging to us at all, but to "Another", i.e. to God. What he calls "the true riches", on the other hand, he describes as our very own property. God cannot entrust the true riches of eternal life in all their fullness to those who are not using material wealth in a way which is obedient to his revealed will. In other words, the quality of our spiritual life inevitably reveals the measure of our faithfulness to God over material things. As we prove scrupulously straight with him in our use of money, so he is able to strengthen our faith, deepen our assurance, use our testimony, secure our peace and joy.

The fourth attitude stressed in these verses is: *single-mindedness*. "No servant can serve two masters; for either

he will hate the one and love the other, or he will be
devoted to the one and despise the other. You cannot
serve God and mammon."[12] This brings us right back to
covetousness as idolatry, deliberately breaking the first
and the great commandment, summarised by Jesus himself when addressing the challenge of the Kingdom of
God to one on the brink of discipleship: "The Lord our
God, the Lord is one; and you shall love the Lord your
God with all your heart, and with all your soul, and with
all your mind, and with all your strength."[13]

Jesus had to face exactly this temptation from Satan in
the wilderness when he was offered all the kingdoms of
the world, together with their authority and glory: "If
you, then, will worship me, it shall all be yours."[14] Those
are the issues at stake in this conflict: either we worship
the Creator God, or we worship one of his creatures.
Such a life-or-death battle demands utter single-
mindedness, following the same route as Jesus walked in
replying to Satan with the words, "It is written, 'You
shall worship the Lord your God, and him only shall you
serve.'"[15]

Losing our fear

Contentment and joyful sharing are the twin marks of
such single-minded Christians who, with complete scrupulousness, use their material possessions shrewdly and
strategically for the Kingdom of God. In this way "unrighteous mammon" is redeemed to become part of a
whole life style that manifests the unshakeable Kingdom
of God. The spirit of contented sharing is an authentic
Christian hallmark. It comes from taking with trusting
seriousness the promise of God: "I will never fail you nor
forsake you."[16] The problem, once again, is fear – fear of
what will happen if we truly share in the unstinting way
demonstrated by Jesus. But the conclusion of the writer
to the Hebrews is clear: "We can confidently say, 'The
Lord is my helper; I will not be afraid; what can man do to
me?'"[17] As elsewhere in the Scriptures, we are urged to

take a resolute stand against such actual fears: when God says "Fear not", we decide "I will not be afraid".

Some of the most moving and important experiences in my life have been, I believe, in meeting and receiving from Christians who have learned to be content with the minimum and to share it with others. In southern Chile in 1976 I visited a rural area which had seen a revival of a remarkable kind, with virtually a whole community turning overnight from animism to Christ. I was welcomed as a Christian brother from overseas, who had flown in the sky in a metal bird, and given the red-carpet treatment. This, for peasants who lived on herb-tea, vegetables and occasional fruit, amounted to providing a special bowl of carefully preserved sugar to sweeten the communal *maté*, or tea. The vibrant faith and love of these very poor Chileans was contagious.

I was privileged to receive such generous hospitality from other greatly-impoverished Christians in Uganda in 1981. Their desperate straits and their violent situation seem to kindle, rather than to quench, the simmering fires of joyful discipleship. Is this what James meant when he asked: "Has not God chosen those who are poor in the world to be rich in faith and heirs of the Kingdom which he has promised to those who love him?"[18]

Because most readers of this book will not be in such compulsorily-deprived situations, it is important to take a final look at the question of a sharing life style in the light of four specific aspects of Christian discipleship – fasting, tithing, community-living and expecting the return of Jesus in glory which will mark the termination of this world-order as we know it.

When you fast

Invariably in the New Testament fasting is linked with prayer, and the two practices are not to be undertaken in order to be seen by others.[19] A good clue, however, to our willingness to trim our life style for the sake of the Kingdom of God can be found in our reactions to a call to prayer over a longish period of time, including normal meal times. Very often it is the call of the physical appetites which transcends the call to prayer. As individual Christians we know this to be pervasively true with sleep; corporately, we need from time to time to respond to the urgency or intractability of a particular situation with prayer and fasting. The time spent in preparing, consuming and recovering from most meals is very great: this is the time which Jesus envisaged our using creatively for such spiritual discipline. Are we ready to share ourselves in this way for the sake of others?

Tithing

Tithing has been the subject of much debate over the years: is it a New Testament pattern or principle for giving, or not? Ignoring the specifics of the debate, we can still ask ourselves how we react to any summons to tithe our income and our possessions. If there is a resistance in our hearts to such a call, we probably ought to question our readiness to share what we have. The Christian who is gripped by the love of Christ will not be asking "How little can I give?" but "How much can I give?" or rather "How little do I need for myself so that I can give the rest away?"

The bottom-line for Christian giving remains the example set by Macedonian believers in extreme poverty: "Their joy was so great that they were extremely generous in their giving, even though they are very poor. I can assure you that they gave as much as they could, and even more than they could. Of their own free will they begged us and pleaded for the privilege of having a part in helping God's people in Judea. It was more than we could have hoped for! First they gave themselves to the Lord; and then, by God's will they gave themselves to us as well."[20] "First they gave themselves" – that is Christian giving, and such 100 per cent giving will include at least 10 per cent of our income.

Living under the same roof

The impetus towards living-in-community has some-
what abated in the last five years or so. It still remains a
good touchstone of our willingness for "doing good and
sharing what we have". When we as a family faced up to
the possible call of God to such a life style, we found that
our basic attitudes came under painful scrutiny. One or
two of our close friends in Cape Town decided to live
together in community, under the same roof and having
virtually all things in common. We chose to have as open
a home as possible (which invariably means a rather
more comprehensive sharing for the pastor of a local
church than for the ordinary layman), to be ready to have
people to stay as members of the family for as long as was
right. In the last six years this has involved us in having
several different people for three months or so at a time.
It has meant having elderly relatives for a couple of years.
It has led to having a single person live with us open-
endedly and staying for a year. It has also meant welcoming a Tanzania-bound missionary, together with his ten-
year-old son, for a couple of nights while his entry visas
arrived – and having them for nearly three months! In
each case, we have been immensely blessed, thoroughly
stretched, and regularly challenged by the experience. It
has been good, from time to time, to put up the shutters
and relax together as an "ordinary" family. Are we ready
for such sharing?

Fasting, tithing, living-in-community: none of these
are of the essence of what it is to be Christian; but each
has the knack of touching us on the raw. The verses from
Hebrews at the beginning of this chapter see such a
sharing life style as full of "sacrifices". If, on the other
hand, they are "pleasing to God", that should provide all
the incentive we need to press on with more costly
discipleship.

Jesus will return

This becomes crucial when we remind ourselves that
Jesus is returning one day in great glory to claim his full

inheritance and to wind up this present world-order. What is our genuine and most profound reaction to such a certainty? If everything we now possess were to disappear tomorrow, where would our hearts turn out to reside? "For where your treasure is, there will your heart be also."[21]

Is the local church prepared to set the pace in such sharing? A shared life means a simplified life style. We need one another to discover ways of trimming our standard of living, and so to cock a snook at the acquisitive society in which we live. As a church thus emerges from the cess-pit of materialism, it will in no sense endorse any boorish elimination of beauty and creativity; but it will release resources for different needs as God stresses one here, one there. Perhaps by his Spirit he will motivate us to set members of our church free for specialist ministry, or to support an overseas or local worker, or to establish new ministry to those in need, or simply to make money available for the disaster-areas of the world.

We are, in this as in every area, to walk the road Jesus walked. He said of himself: "Foxes have holes and the birds of the air have their nests; but the Son of man has nowhere to lay his head"[22] – and he said it in response to a man like ourselves who said: "I will follow you wherever you go."[23]

7 Shared leadership

"Remember your leaders, those who spoke to you the word of God; consider the outcome of their life, and imitate their faith . . . Obey your leaders and submit to them; for they are keeping watch over your souls, as men who will have to give account. Let them do this joyfully, and not sadly, for that would be of no advantage to you."[1]

By this stage it is inevitable that we find ourselves asking questions about the kind of leadership required if a local church is going to press ahead in the direction we have been considering. The writer of the Hebrews verses quoted above clearly has in mind a team of leaders to whom the membership can look with confidence: he urges them, not merely to remember their leaders but to obey them and submit to them. In the first verse he seems to have in mind those who first declared God's word to them, but who have probably died. In the second verse he has in mind their present leadership. If we conflate the two cameos, we have an interesting picture of local church leadership.

First, leadership comes from those who speak to the people the word of God. This conforms precisely to Paul's priorities for an overseer (Greek: *episkopos* or "bishop"): "he must hold firm to the sure word as taught, so that he may be able to give instruction in sound doctrine and also to confute those who contradict it."[2] The ability adequately to handle the Scriptures is cardinal to the ministry of leadership in a local church.

Secondly, the writer to the Hebrews urges his readers to consider closely "the outcome of their life": he is asking them to observe the kind of character they showed – was it consistently Christ-honouring? Were they in control of their families, their tongues, their temper, their eating and drinking habits?[3] It does not matter in the end how competent a teacher of the Bible a person may be, if his manner of life contradicts his teaching.

Thirdly, the stress is placed unequivocally on the need to "imitate their faith". Leaders are meant by God to blaze a trail in living and operating from faith. Faith necessarily includes taking risks and launching out into the deep. It means sailing in uncharted seas and quietly moving ahead into the unknown – because God says so. There is a wise caution in leadership, but there is also bold faith. In a local church we need to imitate not the gifts or the quirks or the behaviour of those in leadership, but their faith.

Fourthly, leadership involves "keeping watch over your souls". There is a special responsibility involved in spiritual oversight: leaders are called not merely to be alert to the spiritual needs of each person in their care, but to remember that one day they will have to give account to God himself for the way they have exercised their ministry. Obviously, no man can ever take such responsibility upon himself: he must be called to it by God so that he can also be equipped for it by God.

A local team ministry

If these four aspects of leadership – i.e. declaring God's word, living consistently, setting an example of faith, and alert oversight – are essential in the life of a local church, it is obvious that such an onerous responsibility must be shared. This is the consistent perspective of the New Testament. For example, when Paul left Titus in Crete, he gave him explicit instructions to "amend what was defective" in the church. How was Titus to do this? By appointing "elders in every town as I directed you".[4] The church in Crete was defective – the word refers to things missing which prevented the Church being what

God intended. An essential part of the remedy was to find responsible Christians in every local church to exercise oversight. In other words, this oversight was to be both corporate and indigenous, a local team-ministry. This was clearly Paul's regular custom in the churches of the Mediterranean basin, if Luke's account of the apostolic practice in Asia Minor is anything to go by – "when [Paul and Barnabas] had appointed elders for them in every church, with prayer and fasting, they committed them to the Lord in whom they believed."[5]

It is important to appreciate how far we have moved from this pattern in today's Church. By contrast we have perpetuated a system of ministry in which selection, training, appointment and practice are all highly suspect, if not plainly wrong. In the main, we take young men, with scarcely no experience of the harsh realities of pastoral oversight but with enthusiasm and a sense of vocation; we send them off to a college or seminary for three or four years of what, with the best will in the world, is essentially an academic training under tutors who are often as inexperienced in pastoral oversight as themselves; they are then removed to a church in an area far away from their home territory, and put in sole charge of an unsuspecting congregation, usually after a short trial run under a senior minister. After a period of more or less "successful" ministry, they are then transferred to another church, and the process begins again.

Pastoral responsibility in the New Testament is always shared. The only recognised difference in ministry is between local and itinerant, and the itinerant ministry is normally subject to the authority of the local oversight. Quite apart from the positive gains of working in this way, all the necessary safeguards are built in – safeguards against rash or premature decisions, against heavy leadership and dominant personalities, against loneliness and depression, against the development of a professional clergyman who becomes the cork in the bottle of real growth.

If local teamwork is to flourish, the present minister must surely recognise his call to be a trainer of others for the work of ministry. This will necessarily involve his sharing not just his gifts and his insights but himself as a person with those whom God has placed around him. As he does this they will begin to appreciate the strains and stresses of pastoral oversight. These will be an eye-opener to most lay members of a congregation. Gradually a team will emerge of people who really know and trust one another, who share one another's lives and are able to minister together. Each will have different gifts, and the distinctive contribution of each will come to be recognised and valued. When the time comes for one of them, the ordained person or not, to move on, the ministry is maintained – not as an interim arrangement, but as a team.

Where does the buck stop?

For a team to function at all, let alone with its proper potential, it seems inevitable that there must be one person who carries the can and has ultimate executive responsibility. This is certainly the way of the world, but in the Church (particularly a local church) we have tended to accept this model uncritically. What, after all, does it mean for Jesus Christ to be head of his body? If there is one person in a local church who has the last word, have we not at that moment wrenched the leadership from the Lord and entrusted it to a mere human being? Is such mimicry of the unbelieving world really the Christian way to behave?

At the very least, we must surely accept that leadership in the New Testament is not a matter of status or seniority, but of *charisma*, or a gift of God's grace. Indeed, if we take the broad sweep of biblical teaching on the nature of Christian leadership, we are forced to ask very searching questions of the way it is currently exercised in all sections of the Church. We certainly seem to be past the era of autocratic bishops and senior ministers. Local pastors and vicars are rarely able today to enforce their own wills on congregations, not at any rate by virtue of their position – although some manage it by force of personality and manipulation. On the other hand, the more accepted versions of Christian leadership in vogue today also veer very perilously towards the ever-present danger of lording it over the flock.[6]

In one particular house-fellowship in North London I heard of a striking example of this kind of domineering oversight. A young couple, recently married and only aged 22, had responsibility as "elders" for a group of Christians, many of whom were considerably older than themselves. The man was visiting one of his "flock" and found the dishes lying dirty in the kitchen. He saw it as his task as an elder to reprimand the person for slovenliness. This is just one example of many similar actions which add up to an attempt to run another person's life.

The basis for this attitude to leadership is a complete misreading of the New Testament, which assumes that those appointed elders have an authority inherent in their office. This approach entirely ignores the true nature of Christian leadership, as modelled by Jesus and expounded by the biblical writers. The nub of this is service. The most authoritative person in the Christian community is the most willing and consistent servant of all.[7] On this basis, the young North London elder would have demonstrated a God-given *charisma* of leadership by washing up the dirty dishes, not by taking the poor girl to task.

When Christians notice brothers or sisters who thus lay down their lives in service for the community, they want to respect, obey and submit to them. In other words, Christian submission is not a duty to be imposed but an attitude which is spontaneously undertaken in response to sacrificial love. There is a fascinating little insight into the true nature of such leadership towards the end of Paul's first letter to the church at Corinth[8] – an important detail because there were those at Corinth who liked to impose a very heavy leadership on God's people. Here Paul says this: "The household of Stephanas . . . have devoted themselves to the service of the saints; I urge you to be subject to such men and to every fellow worker and labourer." C. K. Barrett sees these words as

the earliest reference to what eventually became formal-
ised as the ministry of the Church.[9] If Barrett is correct,
we see precisely what Christian leadership is meant to
portray – a spirit of self-sacrifice in serving others in the
family of God.

Discovering God's will

The implications of this truth are radical, both for the
choice of leadership in the local church and for the way
we make decisions about God's will for his people. Such
criteria as secular gifts, articulacy, education, warm personalities and the like take a very low place on our list of
priorities. The qualities highlighted in the pastoral epistles leap to the forefront. The gifts we will be concerned to
bring forward will be spiritual endowments for enabling
the ministry of the Church.

Paul sees these enabling ministries as essentially five in
number: the apostles, the prophets, the evangelists, the
pastors and the teachers.[10] A local team-leadership will
include each of these. The apostolic ministry stresses the
need to break new ground; a prophet takes time quietly
to stand in the council of God, and then declares what
he hears without fear or favour; the evangelist will constantly be out with unbelievers and will therefore be
looking at the life of the Church through their eyes; the
pastor will be sensitive to the needs of individuals and
the way decisions affect them; the teacher will be concerned to build up the Church in God's word. Each
distinctive perspective is needed if the team (and therefore the local church) is not going to be unbalanced,
either settling down into boring conformity or turning
into a holy huddle or becoming packed with information
but short on real growth.

Because we so often fail to have the correct attitude to
choosing leadership in a local church, we inevitably tend
to bumble along in our decision-making. My own experience, as a participating member of five active local
churches in the last twenty years, has made me in-

creasingly convinced that we have it fundamentally wrong when it comes to discerning the will of God.

Leaving on one side the propriety of voting democratically at an annual general meeting for our representatives on the Church Council (or equivalent body), is it really right to conduct God's work like a business meeting, with a Christian version of chairman, minutes, agenda, matters arising and any other business? What is the quality of relationships like in such a gathering? Does anybody truly know the others in the room? Is a monthly meeting at the end of a tiring day the best way to proceed? Is Jesus Christ really the Head of such decision-making? Do less articulate and less quick-witted members have a proper chance to function? Even if we claim to move ahead only on the unanimity principle, do such meetings actually produce genuine unanimity? Are there not always unconvinced, if not dissenting, voices in the church carpark afterwards? Is unanimity, anyway, the determinative principle for a group of Christians? Can we not all be sincerely and unanimously wrong?

We are probably not as aware as we might be of the treadmill of meetings in today's world. It has been calculated that about 400 million people – approximately one tenth of all humanity – go to a meeting every day of the year.[11] "You can bet a chairman's gavel to three well-chewed pencils that almost everyone leaves moaning that it's all been a waste of time. None the less, they will all turn up at the next one – meetingolics desperate for a fix."

In analysing ordinary meetings of this kind in the secular world, Winston Fletcher explains the disease of meetingolism as that suffered by those who attend meetings because they hate being left out of things; because they are scared of decisions being taken in their absence; because it makes them feel important; because they want a rest from their real work; because they want to offload the responsibility for a difficult decision; because they particularly like the sound of their own voices; or – most frequently of all – simply because the meeting happens to be happening.

These factors are so commonly, if not universally, present in Christian meetings that we need to take a long hard look at the determinative influences at work on such occasions. Have we ever developed a biblically sound and consistent approach to such dynamics? This becomes even more important when we absorb Fletcher's "seven deadly skills of meeting manipulation" – it only requires a little imagination to see these techniques in operation in any Church Council meeting – aggression, conciliation, enthusiasm, interrogation, patience, sulks and withdrawal.

With his tongue fairly obviously well in his cheek, Fletcher concludes: "To deploy the Seven Deadly Skills successfully, you will need at least a smidgen of theatricality in your blood. With that, and some hard practice, you will soon be able to develop the tricks and the techniques, the ploys and the stratagems – like Hassle the Chairman and Fight the Wrong Fight – with which you can manipulate meetings to your advantage (and have a little fun while you're at it)."

The ecclesiastical version of such meetings looks less and less like the right vehicle for discerning the will of God. We would, presumably, be agreed that what matters is discovering God's will and doing it. The most important thing is that the people God wants to be in shared leadership should be in place, and that they should operate in God's way. There is an important injunction in Paul's priorities for the local church in his letter to the Colossians, when he writes: "Let the peace of Christ rule (literally, "be the referee") in your hearts, to which indeed you were called in the one body."[12] Paul clearly envisages situations in the corporate life of a local church where a determinative and decisive principle needs to be brought into action. He does not envisage this being the person with whom the buck stops; nor does he see it as the will of the majority; he does not regard total unanimity as the key. He speaks of the peace of Christ as the referee.

By this phrase Paul presumably means the peace which Christ gives, of which Jesus himself spoke in his parting words to the disciples: "Peace I leave with you; my peace I give to you; not as the world gives do I give to you."[13] This peace Paul elsewhere describes as "the peace of God, which passes all understanding".[14] The outstanding truth about the peace of Christ, therefore, is that it is a *gift* of the ascended Lord to his people. We cannot ourselves produce that peace, let alone vote it into a meeting. As with all God's gifts, all we can do is to receive them – i.e. to create time and space to make them our own and to cherish them. When those in leadership in a local church are involved in making decisions, they need to wait for God's gift of peace to mark their arrival at his will.

The context of Paul's injunction to the Colossians indicates strongly that such an experience of the peace of Christ is possible only if the circumstances, in which the decisions are being reached, are conducive. For Paul that involves high-quality relationships and submission to the word of God.[15] It is virtually impossible to build good relationships between a group of twenty or thirty people meeting for business on a monthly (at the most) basis. The dynamics of interrelating have to be re-established on each occasion – if, indeed, they are ever in place. Although I have never been able to implement this, I am convinced that a pattern of quarterly away-days (or even weekends) would provide a far more constructive context. In such an atmosphere justice could be done to all the necessary ingredients for such decision-making: worship, study of relevant Scriptures, ministry to one another to clear the decks for discovering God's will, time to let everyone present express both thought-out convictions and instinctive gut-level feelings, praying unhurriedly and thoroughly over the situation, waiting for God to give his peace to confirm that we now have his mind.

Congregational peace

The Colossians perspective also intimates strongly that there is a specific calling to know God's peace for the whole of a local church gathered together. Perhaps it needs a bit more faith on the part of the leadership to take the risk of such congregational meetings at regular intervals in order to air matters of importance which affect the whole body. I have seen this done over large financial issues with great benefit. In Oxford, about three years ago, we were deeply troubled by both the lack of Christian families and the shortage of able people with a vocation to minister to young people, especially teenagers. We held a congregational meeting in the context of Sunday evening worship, at which many constructive points were made on all sides of the situation. It took about nine months to have any obvious results, but the overall impact (as observable now) has been quite remarkable. At the meeting there was, by the end of the discussion, a notable sense of Christ's peace assuring us that he would secure the work of the church with Christian families.

Such congregational meetings both promote and indicate genuine trust between the leadership and membership of a local church. There is always a tendency for those in leadership, however representative and corporate, to get out of touch with the way ordinary people in the church are thinking and feeling.

Greater openness and a spirit of mutually supportive service are essential if Christian leadership is not to degenerate into a destructive grind. Far too many Christians are, quite simply, worn out by too much unsupported and isolated burden-bearing. If those in oversight of the local church are to "do this joyfully, and not sadly",[16] they must not be allowed to operate as soloists.

In the last ten years or so, I have tried to make such team-leadership a top priority in three successive churches. These teams have included men and women, ordained and lay people, singles and married couples, people of different ages but all with considerable experience as Christians. I have worked – and continue to work – in close partnership both with my "professional" colleagues in so-called full-time ministry, and with Christians in secular occupations of different kinds who give themselves in their spare time to such leadership in their local church. I am totally convinced that this is not merely a good way to operate but the only biblical approach to Christian leadership.

This is not to say that it is not very painful, arduous and often frustrating. If you are a certain kind of articulate person, trained and educated to take decisions by yourself and stand on your own two feet, it is much simpler to run it all yourself and to keep people relatively happy by mobilising them in different kinds of subsidiary ministry. But, despite the aches and pains of shared leadership, I would never return to the old style of ministry.

Such a pattern has meant that I have had to revise my own priorities in daily ministry. I suppose I spend up to one-third of my working time meeting with different members of the team in Oxford, not really for business but to share together as Christians. I try to spend up to an hour with each one at least once a fortnight: in a fair-sized church, that means a large chunk of time; but it is crucial if we are to work together genuinely as a team. I know of many churches which talk about team-ministry and let it be known that they operate as a team – but the hard facts are that the team scarcely ever meets except for business, and even that necessity often goes by default.

It would be wrong for me to give the impression that the teams in which I have been involved have always been effective in joint ministry. All the obvious problems hit the surface sooner or later, especially confusion in the congregation about the locus of actual leadership. If those sharing such responsibility are not keeping close to one another, these uncertainties will abound and bring nothing but division and party spirit. One leader will be set against another with unerring precision. The pernicious character of such an attitude is that neither the relevant leaders nor those responsible for such polarisation will necessarily be aware of what is happening.

These – and many similar – realities reinforce in many sceptics the conviction that, as in the world, so in a church the buck must stop on someone's desk, not with a team. I do not believe this is so. Provided that nobody on the team pulls rank or swings status with the others, it is perfectly possible to work together under the overall headship of Jesus himself. I admit this is a very considerable proviso, because Christian leaders are all too human and can easily revert to a defiant "I'm the Vicar" approach when uncertain or feeling eclipsed. If, however, the relationships on the team are sound and open, it ought to be possible to point out any such refuge of frightened or self-assertive men.

If leadership is a matter of spiritual *charismata*, not status, a local church team ought to reflect the multifaceted ministry described by Paul in Ephesians 4:11, and to operate in accordance with the varied contributions there outlined. In his book, *You are my God*, David Watson describes the distinctive tensions inherent in such local team-ministry.[17] He concludes that, in an Anglican parish for example, the Rector or Vicar has a role parallel to Timothy's position when left by Paul in charge of the church at Ephesus. He sees the Rector/Vicar as having some kind of apostolic authority on the Ephesus model. I believe this is a faulty and a dangerous analogy because apostolic authority is vested today not in particular people but in the apostolic teaching contained in the Scriptures.

No, such a conclusion as David Watson's seems to me another example of unconsciously and subtly easing Jesus out of genuine headship of his Church in the day-to-day realities of a local church. As the Head he gives individuals to his Church with the particular gifts required to equip God's people for the work of ministry. As they employ their gifts in sacrificial service, the whole body is enabled to proclaim the Kingdom of God. I do not believe that necessitates one person in overall or final charge.

Our major obstacle is, I think, that we are subconsciously looking for a solution to the problems of leadership – who does not want an easier life, especially in Christian ministry? It is a highly-pressurised calling and we instinctively want to find a way which lets us off at least a few hooks. When shared leadership hits snags and trauma, it is a simple matter to throw in the towel and exclaim, "There you are, it doesn't *work*!"

Does it really matter if it does not *work*? We are called to reflect biblical principles and priorities in Christian ministry, regardless of results. I do not believe the New Testament teaches the need for, let alone the rightness of, one person holding ultimate responsibility. Jesus holds that responsibility – thank God! When, therefore, we disagree as a team, we hold tight to the lordship of Jesus and refuse to opt out into buck-passing to any one individual. Gradually, the team itself – and the congregation as a whole – will learn to listen to the Head's instructions.

The cost of teamwork

Such shared leadership is a challenge not only to the ordained minister. Many committed Christian lay men and women have had to face up to far more costly challenges in order to respond to God's call for them to be involved more fully in the leadership of their local church. I know of one consultant anaesthetist who deliberately and prayerfully turned down a very attractive promotion because he knew that God wanted him to be more involved in pastoral leadership in his local church. Needless to say, God has abundantly blessed him and his family in and as a result of that courageous decision.

When it comes to married women assuming responsibility in shared leadership, there is only one major warning that ought to be stressed. Very often a Christian wife is a long way ahead of her husband in spiritual maturity. It is a great temptation to hurry her into leadership prematurely. Invariably such haste widens the gap between her and her husband. It is far wiser – and also does far more justice to two, admittedly very difficult, passages in Paul's letters[18] – to wait for him to catch up spiritually before bringing them both together into leadership. This is true of home-church leadership as much as the wider context of the local church.

Any discussion today of leadership in a local church needs to conclude with a renewed focus on Jesus Christ as the Head of his body. That is presumably the reason why the writer to the Hebrews follows his reference to their leaders with the bald, but compelling, assertion that "Jesus Christ is the same yesterday and today and for ever."[19] Modern personality cults and counselling techniques both make it necessary to reiterate the supreme pre-eminence of Jesus as Lord of his Church. We cannot afford to run the risk of human beings (one alone or several in a team) imperceptibly side-lining the King of kings.

He himself taught this explicitly in confronting the archetypal up-front religious leaders of his day – the Pharisees. He insisted that nobody must call another human being, or be called, either Teacher, Father or Guide.[20] Only God – Father, Son and Holy Spirit – can provide the authority, the life and the guidance we all need. He uses men and women, with gifted ministries, in teaching and evangelism and counselling; but we are "all brethren" and we must steadfastly resist the temptation to play God with one another. Any pattern of or approach to leadership which does not start, continue and finish with humble service will founder. God, who is a jealous God, will see to that; and that is why Jesus concludes this warning about the Pharisees with the following words: "He who is greatest among you shall be your servant; whoever exalts himself will be humbled, and whoever humbles himself will be exalted."[21]

That kind of leadership is Christ's gift to his Church. It will remain steady and unshakeable in the fiercest persecution and in the most traumatic experiences. Such leadership we will support readily in prayer, encouragement and loyal respect.

8 Sound teaching

*"Do not be led away by diverse and strange teachings;
for it is well that the heart be strengthened by grace,
not by foods, which have not benefited their
adherents."*[1]

Soon after I was ordained, I went on a training course run
by the College of Preachers, along with about twenty
others in the same position. Each of us had to preach a
sermon in front of the others, and it had to be one which
we had recently preached in our home church. The
critique made by those responsible for the course was
thorough, shrewd and often hard for brash young
preachers to swallow. I remember the most penetrating
and painful remark made about my sermon was: "Where
is the Gospel, the good news, in what you are saying?"

It was a timely and incisive evaluation. Since then I
have tried to ensure that, in regularly expounding the
Bible to the local church week by week, each sermon is
clearly rooted in the good news of what God has done in
Christ. My wife also cajoles me into being less aggressive
and more compassionate than I would otherwise be. My
own evaluation of such regular teaching indicates that it
is very easy to slip into exhortation without explanation
of our rich resources in Christ, to lay heavy burdens on
God's people which produce a sense of failure and sheer
depression. Rightly, preachers hold out the call of God
for us to be holy; but wrongly, the path of holiness
becomes a marathon of effort, slog and achievement (or
failure).

As far as the message of this book is concerned, a

similar danger is always just around the corner. It is one
thing to point out areas in the life of a church which might
have strayed from biblical patterns; it is quite another
thing to point a way forward which is full of hope and
faith. But unless there is that encouragement, the book
ends up being another hammer-blow producing self-
condemnation and failure. That is why it seems to me so
important to see that the unshakeable things in the
Kingdom of God are clearly his *gifts* to his Church, and
that Jesus Christ himself, the King of the Kingdom,
remains unchangeably the same. "Fear not, little flock,
for it is your Father's good pleasure to give you the
Kingdom."[2]

The danger of turning the message of the Gospel into
yet another "do-your-best" philosophy seems at this
stage to occupy the mind of the writer of this letter to the
Hebrews. He throws out a strong warning about the
"diverse and strange teachings" which can so easily lead
God's people into byways of futility and frustration. The
specific character of these teachings is probably impossible to decipher at this distance, but they were clearly
some brand of legalism of a particularly Jewish kind.
They apparently emphasised externals ("foods") rather
than "the heart". Virtually all false teaching in the
Church, whether then or now, veers either in the direction of licence or legalism. David Pawson has used a vivid
illustration to stress that walking in the Spirit is like
walking along a narrow footpath in the hills, with the bog
of legalism on one side and the ravine of licence on the
other.

The grace of God

The value of this passage in the letter to the Hebrews is
that it extricates two essential characteristics of truly
sound teaching and holds them before us with unmistakable clarity – the grace of God and the atoning work
of Jesus Christ. Unless the teaching in a local church is
founded irretrievably upon these two essentials, God's
people will shrivel and die.

There is no substitute for such steady, thorough exposition of God's grace in a local church. Unless there is this consistent diet of sound teaching, believers will not be strengthened for the costly life of faith to which all Christians are necessarily called at the end of the twentieth century. If such unfolding of the grace of God is *not* done, a congregation becomes prey to any forceful or articulate personality who will either cajole or bully them into what he thinks a church ought to be and to do.

Put more bluntly, no preacher or minister can tell a congregation how to behave and what to do. If Christians are not freely motivated by God's grace in Jesus Christ, their activity is not (in any real sense) Christian. Many apparently Christian activities may take place in their local church. It might well have a reputation for being "alive", but God looks for the spontaneous motivation of a heart responding out of gratitude for his grace, not to please another human being.

It is, at the same time, important to stress that a Christian's spontaneous gratitude to God is a matter primarily of the will, not of the feelings. Because God has loved me so unconditionally in Jesus Christ, I decide to present my body to him as a living sacrifice – whether at the moment I feel like it or not. Other Christians, particularly those who have been entrusted by God with the pastoral care of me, may be used to liberate or to activate my will in a specific direction. But they must neither lay heavy burdens on me nor induce a guilty conscience in me if I do not fall in with their wishes or ideas.

There is an inordinate amount of such religious bullying by the "professionals". The task of the teacher/preacher is to lead Christians into a richer appreciation of God's grace. From such an appreciation they will want to serve the Lord with all their ransomed powers. It is presumably obvious that mere head-knowledge of divine grace is not adequate. To know about the grace of God *is* essential, but it is equally vital to provide the opportunity for such knowledge to work itself out in daily life and experience.

I was recently hearing about a married woman with

three teenage children who, having been a committed Christian for twenty years or so, felt that at the age of forty-five there was not much else in life to look forward to. A fundamental reason for this turns out to be the absence in her local church of any pastoral context (i.e. of some kind of more intimate home gathering) for working out "the doctrines of grace" which she hears in the preaching Sunday by Sunday. There seem to be large numbers of Christians who have similarly "plateaued" in their spiritual life. Frequently the remedy for such inertia is exposure to the deep needs, spiritual and other, of neighbours and friends – without any recourse to the "experts" and therefore being compelled to jump in at the deep end trusting in the resources of God's grace to meet such needs.

There are many "diverse and strange teachings" abroad today, especially in the age of the tape-recorder. They generally have some kind of basis in the Scriptures, but they bring God's people into bondage. We need to bring them all under the scrutiny of these two search-lights: do they declare "the manifold grace of God"?[3] Are they rooted and grounded in the Cross of Christ? The sanctifying work of being made holy, like Jesus, is from beginning to end the responsibility of God: by his grace he works in us by his Spirit, applying to us the fruit of Christ's death; "Jesus . . . suffered outside the gate in order to sanctify the people through his own blood."[4]

Over the years I have seen numerous occasions in churches where God's Spirit is clearly at work, when the spiritual life has been diverted away from these central truths. The diversionary tactics are varied, but they normally take something which is good and important in the life of any church, but then turn them from peripherals into essentials. I have witnessed it over healing, deliverance from demonic powers, tithing, fasting, living-in-community, baptism, prophecy, speaking in tongues, patterns of leadership, styles of worship, unanimity in decision-making. If this seems a strongly "charismatic" list of potentially divisive issues, I should add that I have also seen similar problems over matters like hairstyles, dress, smoking and drinking, dancing, modern music, the cinema and the theatre. If that list seems rather antiquated, there is a more subtle legalism which leads to Christians being in bondage to what others think or say – an attitude which inevitably concentrates on external behaviour rather than inner integrity before God.

Another legalism

There is another form of legalism which regards genuine Christianity as determined by whether or not specific issues are on the top of a church's agenda – issues like racialism, unemployment, nuclear disarmament, women's rights, ecology, poverty and the Third World. Enough has been said in this book to indicate that such matters are essential to a relevant, practical and obedient witness to Christ in the world today. But it is absolutely vital that these are tackled in a clearly Christian way, i.e. in the resources of God's grace and demonstrably as a fruit of God's work in reconciling the world to himself in the death of his Son. When the Church gets involved in such issues without being grounded in such a spirituality it is doing nothing intrinsically Christian. The letter to the Hebrews actually provides a unique exposition of the significance of the Cross.[5] This leads me to stress some of the ways in which more emphasis and content can be applied to the theme of the Cross.

One of the regular customs to which most Anglicans are exposed is the Three Hours' Service of meditation on Good Friday. Over the years I have found this concentrated exposure to the meaning of Christ's death to be of the greatest personal benefit. On most occasions I have been entrusted with the immense privilege of actually bringing this teaching. It may be helpful to indicate some of the ways in which the significance of Christ's death can thus be unfolded.

Apart from the more obvious ways – such as the Seven Words from the Cross ("Father, forgive them . . .",[6] "I thirst";[7] "It is finished"[8] etc.) and the actual Passion narratives according to the four Gospels – it is fascinat-

ing to examine the events through the eyes of leading
actors in the drama. Examples could include Pilate,
Barabbas, Joseph of Arimathea, Caiaphas, the two
Marys, the two dying criminals, the soldiers, Simon of
Cyrene. A more exegetical approach would take passages from Paul's epistles which expound the theme of
the Cross. We had a very moving service, one Good
Friday in Cape Town, based on the references to the
Lamb in the Book of Revelation: the wrath of the Lamb,
the blood of the Lamb, the Lamb's book of life, the song
of the Lamb, the marriage-supper of the Lamb, the wife
of the Lamb, the throne of the Lamb.

I remember also another Good Friday when we looked
thoroughly at Psalm 22, the one which begins "My God,
my God, why hast thou forsaken me?" and which was
clearly at the centre of Jesus's own consciousness while
on the Cross. The movement of the psalm seems to
encompass the experience of the Saviour in his last three
hours, and its message encapsulates many aspects of his
redemptive death. There are, in fact, indicators that other
psalms were either on the lips or certainly in the mind of
Jesus at this time (for example, psalms 68 and, perhaps,
31 and 55).

The more imaginative and committed our determination to appreciate the death of Jesus, the more we will
draw from the inexhaustible reservoir of God's lavish
grace to sinful humanity. In the Cross of Christ there is
forgiveness, redemption, atonement, victory over the
forces of evil and death itself, an inspiration to endure
suffering, an example of selfless love as the climax to a
spotless life, and an open door into the very heart of God.
Those who gathered in Jerusalem on that fateful day
illustrate different facets in the significance of Christ's
death. As we watch their behaviour we see mirrored
ourselves and our own contemporaries: these portraits
bring light to what the Reformers rejoiced to call "the
doctrines of grace" – i.e. God's sovereign love and wisdom in choosing, calling, justifying, sanctifying, perfect-
ing and glorifying sinners without any regard to their
merits or any other human criteria of judgment.

Given the importance of such teaching about the grace of God and the meaning of Christ's death, how is it to be brought into the lives of God's people in a local church? It is obvious from the New Testament that God gives teachers to his Church, to each church.[9] This ministry carries abnormally heavy responsibilities – "Let not many of you become teachers, my brethren, for you know that we who teach shall be judged with greater strictness."[10] There is, then, a special calling to teach God's Word, and it is not surprising that the first apostles felt the urgency of this calling so profoundly that they ensured that their local church released them from other responsibilities. Only with such freedom could they devote themselves unstintingly to "prayer and the ministry of the Word" because it was totally wrong for them to "give up preaching the Word of God to serve tables".[11]

Release the teachers

One of the first tasks of the local church is to release its teachers. That will often require a measure of ruthlessness, especially if the ordained minister has the gift of teaching. He has been so conditioned, by his training and by his people's expectations, to be involved in a variety of tasks that he will at first wonder how to fill his days. We must ask ourselves how seriously we believe in the need for sound teaching, if we are not prepared to prune in this way.

Once the teachers have been released to concentrate on the ministry of the Word, they should be given their head. They have no inherent authority because of their office or calling; their authority lies entirely in the authority of God's Word as they faithfully expound it. What they say must always be weighed by the overall teaching of the Scriptures. If the teachers are expected to teach the congregation on a regular basis, we must ask ourselves how much such teaching is actually reaching the lives of the people. In our Western culture, most of us are inured to absorbing information into our minds. We are fairly well-informed about a multiplicity of affairs, but much of it has no bearing on our daily living.

When the amassing of information is not simply to do with more or less interesting facts and figures, but a matter of hearing and responding to the Word of God, we cannot afford to be complacent. James warns us bluntly about the self-deception involved in being purely hearers of God's Word, and not doers.[12] Jesus takes the warning one step further: in his application of the parable of the sower he describes the different pressures which prevent God's Word producing the desired results – the direct action of Satan, the power of temptation, the cares, riches and pleasures of life. Bearing the fruit God intends requires listening, understanding, receiving, holding fast and obeying the Word. Jesus then concludes: "Take heed then how you hear; for to him who has will more be given, and from him who has not, even what he thinks that he has will be taken away."[13]

Apply the teaching

Jesus is plainly warning us that failure to put the teaching we hear into practice leads to spiritual regression. It does not matter how much teaching we absorb in our minds: if we do not obey, we lose even what we assume we have – a judgment which, in the West today, arguably explains much of the comparative ineffectiveness of the Church, which has clearly lost ground over the last two centuries or so. This is such a serious diagnosis that we must discover effective ways of ensuring that Sunday's teaching touches and changes the lives of God's people. The most useful way of achieving this is deliberately to link the Sunday teaching with the life of the home-churches throughout the week.

In Oxford, for example, we did this over a period of nine months with the material which originally formed the skeleton outline for this book. The material was made available to our home-groups, together with biblical passages for study and leading questions for discussion. One theme was dealt with each month, as preachers taught on a different aspect from week to week. We used some audio-visual material produced on each theme by members of the church. At the end of the nine-month period it was commonly felt, in the church as a whole, that we had made large strides together towards God's goal for us. In fact, most home-groups wanted to spend longer on each theme because in applying the teaching they found so much practical obedience was necessary – and that always takes time and patience in mutual encouragement.

This pattern can be followed with any biblical teaching, whether a book, a theme, a character or a general overview. It means that people must be trained to handle such discussions in home-groups. This requires different skills from leading a conventional Bible study: the purpose is not to unlock the meaning of a passage, because this has been done by the preaching on Sunday. The aim is to apply the teaching from Sunday to the daily lives of each member of the home-churches. So the leading question in the home-church will not be, "What does this verse mean?", but "What did God say to you through this passage on Sunday?" Not only does this make attendance on Sunday rather more necessary; it also encourages far more alert attention during the preaching – neither of which can be bad!

In all wisdom

If the two priorities are to release the teachers and apply the teaching, both need to be pursued with vigour by every member of a local church. Paul uses an evocative phrase about this double-barrelled approach to sound teaching. Writing about his own special teaching ministry, he declares: "Him (Jesus) we proclaim, warning every man and teaching every man in all wisdom, that we may present every man mature in Christ. For this I toil, striving with all the energy which he mightily inspires within me."[14] Again we can see the totally absorbing, indeed exhausting, nature of a full-blooded ministry of teaching. It requires unremitting energy and toil, which are possible only through the inspiration of the Holy Spirit who dwells within us. The key phrase in Paul's statement, however, is "warning and teaching every man in all wisdom". The word "warn" (or "admonish") literally means to "drum sense" into people: that requires wisdom. There are many examples of unwise (i.e. sectarian, irrelevant or indigestible) teaching, and we need to take great care over the way we present God's Word.

When Paul summarised his ministry amongst the Christians at Ephesus, he used a number of phrases which illustrate the wisdom of his teaching ministry.[15] The word "testify" comes four times in this farewell speech to the Ephesian elders. The word stresses that a teacher of God's Word is bearing witness to what he has received: he is not concocting his own ideas. Paul testified to "the Gospel of the grace of God",[16] to "repentance to God and . . . faith in our Lord Jesus Christ".[17] He claims that he never once shrank from "declaring to you anything that was profitable"[18] – not palatable, but profitable; nor from "declaring to you the whole counsel of God".[19]

Paul did not pick and choose those parts of the truth of God's Word which he particularly liked or accepted, or which he believed the Ephesians would have appreciated. This full-orbed ministry of "preaching the Kingdom"[20] had involved him in three years' steadfast refusal to "cease night or day to admonish (or 'drum sense into') every one with tears".[21] Perhaps the climax of Paul's address comes when he can claim: "I am innocent of the blood of all of you."[22] Such a teaching ministry throws out a devastating challenge to anyone with a similar calling. At the very least it must compel us to review our application to its demands, particularly asking ourselves whether we are pursuing it "in all wisdom".

I have found that one of the greatest temptations is to adopt a "take it or leave it" attitude: if I do my bit conscientiously, imaginatively and energetically, then it is up to the congregation to put it into practice. Paul's example pins me down here because he saw the teaching ministry in both personal and eternal dimensions. He reckoned "every one"[23] to be his personal responsibility. He could not rest till he had so declared the whole counsel of God, that he could honestly claim to have discharged his responsibility for making plain the issues of life, death and eternity to every individual.

This took Paul nearly three years – which seems not very long, until we remember that he taught daily for about four or five hours in the Hall of Tyrannus for most of that time.[24] Apart from this public teaching ministry in Ephesus, Paul also taught them "from house to house" – a phrase which almost certainly means that Paul went from one home-church to the next. This pattern could well be followed by those gifted in teaching in the local congregation, when some special instruction – perhaps on a theme of current concern – is required over and above the Sunday teaching.

These insights from Paul's farewell speech to the team leadership at Ephesus provide us with many clues to a teaching ministry which was pursued "in all wisdom". Precisely the same kind of ministry is needed in the mutual sharing of a local congregation, especially in its home-churches. This is shown by the fact that Paul uses the same phrase to describe the corporate life of the church in Colossae: "Let the word of Christ dwell in you richly, teach and admonish one another in all wisdom."[25] However conscientiously the gifted teacher proclaims Jesus Christ to the best of his ability and to the limits of his vision, the congregation has a mutual ministry of teaching to one another. It makes little sense to place the content of these two ministries in separate compartments: hence the wisdom of linking Sunday preaching and teaching with the learning together of home-churches.

In case the drift of this chapter seems to be placing too much weight and importance on a few people – perhaps on only one or two in a local church who can teach God's Word effectively on a Sunday – it is worth stressing a foundational truth about proper home-churches. Not only teachers, but all the other enabling ministries in a local church (as Paul describes them in Ephesians 4 and in 1 Corinthians 12) will be present in embryo in each home-church.[26] The home-church lacks nothing except numbers and we can expect teachers, amongst others, gradually to emerge. This process will be creatively accelerated as those already gifted in teaching gather those with potential around them for instruction and on-the-job training. That is the way the first apostles learned from Jesus, and we need to recapture this approach across the board of Christian ministry before it is buried for ever under the welter of academic learning so predominant in our theological colleges and seminaries.

Sound teaching is one of God's gifts to his Church. The Word of God stands for ever as the unshakeable truth of the Kingdom of God. It is imperative that we release the teachers and apply the teaching "in all wisdom".

9 Shame and suffering

"So Jesus also suffered outside the gate in order to sanctify the people through his own blood. Therefore let us go forth to him outside the camp, and bear the abuse he endured. For here we have no lasting city, but we seek the city which is to come."[1]

One of the strange ways in which our old, lower nature continues to rear its ugly head is that, when we have genuinely tried to follow the Spirit in the path of Christian discipleship, we reckon that we will be trouble-free and able to enjoy life in God's world without pain or problems. As we reach the theme of this last chapter, we may well find ourselves brought up with something of a shock to see "shame and suffering" as one of the authentic marks of being citizens of the Kingdom of God. Surely we are tempted to think that a local church, if it walks the road so far outlined, will be successful, effective and popular.

It is important, therefore, to see that much suffering is a gift from God: "It has been granted to you that for the sake of Christ you should not only believe in him but also suffer for his sake."[2] When we look for happiness and success, we need to realise that we are pandering to ourselves – whereas Jesus made it plain that we must deny ourselves if we are to show ourselves fit to be his disciples.[3] At no stage in our discipleship are we to look for rewards.

The proper attitude is epitomised in other words of Jesus, spoken in the form of a parable: "Suppose one of you has a servant who is ploughing and looking after the sheep. When he comes in from the field, do you tell him to hurry and eat his meal? Of course not! Instead, you say to him, 'Get my supper ready, then put on your apron and wait on me while I eat and drink; after that you may have your meal.' The servant does not deserve thanks for obeying orders, does he? It is the same with you; when you have done all you have been told to do, say, 'We are ordinary servants; we have only done our duty.' "[4]

Prosperity teaching

There is a growing welter of teaching in certain circles which rejects this perspective. Success, health, happiness, prosperity are all seen as expected rights for the children of God's kingdom. This prosperity-teaching gains numerous adherents precisely because it panders to our lower nature. It represents what we want to hear, not what we need to hear. It appeals to two kinds of Christian in particular – to those who enjoy a fairly affluent standard of living and need to rationalise or justify it; and it has understandable attractions for those who have been deprived of life's good things and feel they deserve a better deal. When we realise that most Christians are included within these two groupings, we can appreciate the popularity of such teaching.

I know this to be true because I know my own heart. When I am going through the mill, or have for some time been bearing considerable strain on behalf of others, my lower nature screams to me: "You deserve a break; you have earned it." So my own heart panders to my pride: I think I have worked hard enough to merit God's blessing in some tangible way. Instead of responding with the attitude commanded, not just commended, by Jesus – "We have only done our duty" – I hold my good deeds up before God and effectively tell him to give me a break, a bonus or a blessing.

It does not require much insight to recognise this as a thinly-disguised form of self-interest. Its most serious aspect, however, is the way it undercuts the very foundation of the Gospel of God's grace. At no stage do we deserve anything from God; everything we have is a gift

of his love, completely undeserved.[5] From beginning to
end, from our justification to our glorification, we depend on the grace of God who, out of his great love and
mercy, constantly loads us with daily benefits.[6]

Suffering as integral

When we allow ourselves to think in terms of our merit-
ing God's blessings because of our obedience, spirituality
or patient endurance, we begin to see shame and suffering as alien to our discipleship instead of integral to it.
Peter's first letter to Christians about to face unprecedented shame and suffering frequently makes this
point: "Beloved, do not be surprised at the fiery ordeal
which comes upon you to prove you, as though something strange were happening to you."[7] In line with the
rest of the New Testament, Peter sees such suffering as
necessary, not just to prove the genuineness of our faith
but to purge away the dross and refine the gold in our
characters. We tend to forget that God is concerned with
making us in character like his Son, Jesus, not in making
us happy, healthy and successful.

The rest of the letter to the Hebrews gives the same
picture,[8] and the exhortation from that letter, quoted at
the head of the present chapter, in effect summarises
what has gone before: "Jesus . . . suffered outside the
gate in order to sanctify the people through his own
blood. Therefore let us go forth to him outside the camp,
and bear the abuse he endured".[9] If Jesus himself went
through shame and suffering in order perfectly to demonstrate what it means to be the Son of God, then we
should expect the same. To embrace such abuse we need
the mutual strength of both the local church and the
home-church.

A careful study of Paul's second letter to the Corinthians will yield a healthy perspective on both the suffering and the glory which are equally God's calling for his
people. It is crucial that the Christian Church today
discovers, proclaims and lives by a full-blooded theology
of suffering. We live in a world which is suffering trauma-

tically, but in the West we use every man-made means we can lay our hands on to insulate ourselves from the suffering. We have a suffering God and we serve a suffering Saviour. Furthermore, we belong to a suffering Church. For all these reasons we need to see suffering as intrinsic to our calling and as essentially creative in terms of our destiny.

Paul's most evocative statement on the subject is brief and to the point: "Death is at work in us, but life in you."[10] In the context Paul is describing the intense sufferings to which he has been subjected as a minister of the Gospel, and especially as an apostle of Christ. There were infiltrators at Corinth who claimed to teach with apostolic authority, vindicating their claims with glowing accounts of successful ministry in miracles, healings and other manifestations of power. These "false apostles" sounded very like the leaders of some of the "prosperity churches" of today.

In the main, Paul refuses to counter miracle with miracle. At his best he glories not in his successes but in his weaknesses. In this category he includes not only persecution from those who hate and reject Christ; he also refers to inherent weakness in himself, to circumstances which accentuate his mortality and fragility, and indeed to anything that makes him cling to God in vulnerability. He sees such experiences as "always carrying in the body the death of Jesus".[11] He sees his daily experiences as "always being given up to death for Jesus's sake"[12] – and this continuous sense of vulnerability he sees to be indispensable if other Christians, especially the Corinthians, are going to know the new life of Christ.

In other words, there is no spiritual life and joy for any Christian anywhere unless someone in the front line of the battle is paying the cost of that life in intercession and other costly personal ministry. Is this what Paul means in that mysterious phrase in Colossians: "In my flesh I complete what is lacking in Christ's afflictions for the sake of his body, that is, the Church"?[13]

So therefore weakness and suffering, far from being

alien to the true character of the Church, are indispensable ingredients of growth. They secure us firmly in the dynamics of Calvary and ensure that we daily lay down our lives so that others may live. That Christian is out of step with Jesus who does not know – and, more seriously, who does not *want* to know – the experience of weakness, vulnerability and suffering.

A few examples will help to crystallise this truth.

Several years ago I was present at a retreat for clergy led by the Bishop of the diocese. The traditional expectations for such an occasion stressed the strength, authority and competence of the retreat conductor. The diocese had a history of forceful leadership, which had often been involved in confrontation with secular authorities over national matters of righteousness and compassion. A key moment – for both the retreat and for the spiritual renewal of that diocese and beyond in succeeding years – came in the closing Eucharist, when the Bishop broke down and sobbed virtually uncontrollably for three or four minutes in front of his clergy, confessing his inability, if not unwillingness, to love some of his fellow clergy as much as others.

A similar moment of truth came for the people of St Michael-le-Belfry in a weekend conference in Derbyshire in 1978. During the meeting on Saturday evening David Watson inexplicably broke down in front of his people, who shared his deep depression and vulnerability.

I mention these two occasions not because they necessarily illustrate the Church's calling to suffering but because they illustrate the power released by leaders who share their own suffering and weakness – the power amongst their people to face up to their own sufferings. There seems at times to be what amounts to a conspiracy of adequacy in the Church. Success is seen in terms of not merely coping but conquering in all circumstances. To admit to pain and strain, failure and mistakes, incompetence and inadequacy is regarded as almost culpable and certainly indicative of unworthiness to minister.

The menace of this attitude lies in what it prevents or, at least, quenches, namely the freedom to be open with

one another about the way in which we really feel and
are. I can think of at least three occasions in the last few
years when this has been demonstrated in my own life.
In 1979, when I was about to preach my last sermon in the
church in which we had learned and received so much
over the last seven years or more, I announced my text
and then began to sob. I could not continue for about
three minutes or so during which time my colleagues
came to pray with me in the pulpit. The most memorable
comment on that occasion was made by someone in the
congregation afterwards: "That has bound you to us in
our hearts. We will never forget you."

A second occasion was in Oxford at the end of a series
of talks on Jacob. We were looking at Jacob's sufferings,
explicitly the constant refrain of suffering in his family. I
had recounted seven traumatic experiences in his life of
this kind and it was as though God wanted to express the
reality of his suffering in the suffering of his people as the
God of Jacob; again I broke down and there was a hiatus
of a minute or two. Subsequent events demonstrated two
crucial truths to have been prophetically expressed in
those particular tears: we were due – in the congregation, notably in the central core of leadership – to go
through a time of special suffering; also, God himself was
demonstrating his own weeping heart through my own
tears. There were one or two people in the congregation
who perceived these two things at the time before anything of this nature actually happened.

The third occasion was very different. For over twenty
years I have suffered weakness and pain through slipped
discs in the lumbar region of my back – and "suffered" is
the word at times, as any victims of sciatica will readily
testify. It has been likened to the pain preceding child-
birth, but incessant rather than spasmodic, and nothing
to show for it! At the time of writing I am in the middle of
a particularly vicious bout. It is also a time when very
important decisions have to be taken for our future
ministry and family life. I would dearly love the sciatica to
go away immediately, totally and permanently. In fact, I
have had four sleepless nights because of the pain.

During these night hours God has made his way for our immediate future intensely plain – "pain makes plain" would be a fine summary. For several months, when I have been free from such suffering, the way ahead has remained manifestly obscure. Another side-effect of the back pain happened one recent Sunday evening – I was due to preach but was feeling exhausted through pain and sleeplessness. I told the congregation about this: several came to pray, and I preached sitting down. The power and presence of God were known in the congregation that evening.

Now most people, most Christians, are suffering in one way or another. None of us chooses to suffer: but will we choose to *taste* our sufferings, or even – like Paul – to rejoice and glory in them, "so that the power of Christ may rest"[14] upon us? I have mentioned personal experiences of ministers with those in their pastoral care because it seems true to say that the dynamics of a church's spiritual life are intimately bound up with the spiritual life of its leadership.

As, therefore, the leadership of a church learns to count weakness and suffering as friends, instead of resenting them as intrusions into "successful" ministry,[15] so the members are gradually freed to embrace the implications of authentic discipleship. That will increasingly entail suffering specifically for the sake of Christ, as distinct from the general kind of suffering we have been considering. It is significant that in none of the examples just given was the expression of vulnerability and weakness engineered or compelled. In each case things simply happened – presumably because those concerned did not put any brake on what was welling up inside them under the initiative of God. This active co-operation with God in what he wants to do among us seems to be the essence of walking God's way in suffering of all kinds.

When everything around us is being shaken on the scale we experience today, the Church – when it faithfully reveals God's authentic alternative – will become a special target for abuse and persecution. Jesus himself promised this: "If the world hates you, know that it has hated me before it hated you. If you were of the world, the world would love its own; but because you are not of the world, but I chose you out of the world, therefore the world hates you. Remember the word that I said to you, 'A servant is not greater than his master.' If they persecuted me, they will persecute you; if they kept my word, they will keep yours also. But all this they will do to you on my account . . ."[16]

This is the significance of the emphasis in Hebrews (13:12–14) on suffering "outside the gate" and "outside the camp". In terms of the securities built by godless society, the Christian Church will always be regarded as "outsiders". Instead of trying to be acceptable to those who control "the city" (which often in the Scriptures stands for the world as organised without reference to God),[17] and thereby evading the cost of identifying with the crucified Jesus, we are urged to leave our ghettoes within the city and join him outside.

Rocking the boat

The Bible makes it plain that taking our stance as outsiders will provoke those in authority simply because they are the ones threatened when a minority is out of step with the status quo. Of Jesus it was said that "the common people heard him gladly."[18] James reminds the Christians of his own day: "Is it not the rich who oppress you, is it not they who drag you into court? Is it not they who blaspheme the honourable name which was invoked over you?"[19] The rich and the powerful opposed Jesus and had him eliminated.

To maintain such a witness as outsiders, but with our feet firmly on the ground to prevent isolationism or irrelevance, requires both a hard skin and a proper sense of impermanence. Jesus attributed the hatred of unbelievers to the fact that "I testify of it (i.e. the world) that its works are evil."[20] When we stand up against evil, we will be hated. Such abuse is authentically anti-Christian. The Archbishop of Toledo recently refused to welcome the head of the Spanish government to a celebration of

Corpus Christi in the city because the Church rejects the government's liberal approach to abortion. He had to face considerable invective.

There was one occasion in Cape Town when we, as a church, decided to stand firm against the demolition of squatters' shanties in the middle of a particularly stormy winter. This stance involved our breaking several laws of the land. I discussed the implications of this with a Christian Member of Parliament in the opposition. I still remember his advice: "If it is right to do it, David, do it – and be prepared for the consequences: don't complain about the cost of obedience."

When Christians whine if the godless world abuses them they almost invalidate their initial stance. The testimony of the Scriptures is plain: "If, when you do right and suffer for it, you take it patiently, you have God's approval. For to this you have been called, because Christ also suffered for you, leaving you an example, that you should follow in his steps."[21] So far from advising complaints or protests, Peter urges: "Rejoice in so far as you share Christ's sufferings, that you may also rejoice and be glad when his glory is revealed."[22] He even goes one step further: "If you are reproached for the name of Christ, you are blessed, because the Spirit of glory and of God rests upon you."[23]

This exhortation stands in direct line with the words of Jesus himself: "Blessed are you when men hate you, and when they exclude you and revile you, and cast out your name as evil, on account of the Son of man! Rejoice in that day, and leap for joy, for behold, your reward is great in heaven."[24] This beatitude reminds us also of our true home and our permanent citizenship in the Kingdom of God. As Christians we need to develop a far more profound consciousness that this world is not our home: "here we have no lasting city, but we seek the city which is to come."[25]

The issue of patriotism

It is becoming clearer each day that this theme of
citizenship, nationality and patriotism will become one of
the key issues of Christian discipleship in coming days.
The film *Chariots of Fire* highlighted the alternatives over a
matter with comparatively unimportant consequences –
when Eric Liddell refused on Christian principle to run
in the 1924 Olympic Games' qualifying heats for the
100-yards' sprint, because they were to take place on a
Sunday. One of the film's many memorable scenes
showed Liddell being pressurised by aristocracy and
authority to put King and country before God.

The time is coming when taking a similar stand for the
name of Jesus will involve far more serious consequences
for Christians in the West, as far-reaching as have been
faced by countless believers in other parts of the world for
many years. There still seems to be a strong feeling in
certain Christian circles that disobedience to those in
authority in the country is necessarily wrong. We find
ourselves wondering what would have happened to the
Christian Church if the first Christians – and innumerable 20th-century Christians – had taken such a line.[26]

The main challenge to a local church at this point lies in
its corporate allegiance to the sovereign authority of Jesus
Christ. A Christian community will be able to stand firm
under pressure only as, together, it experiences the
reality of being fellow-citizens of the Kingdom of God. A
local church or a home-church, which intends to make its
mark for Christ in its neighbourhood, will find no shortage of issues on which to take an unequivocal stand for
what is right.

It is not straightforward to combine a sense of impermanence in this world-order with a relevant involvement in our local community. But we cannot afford either
to opt out of our aching world into an escapist separatism
or to invest uncritically in a world-order that is being
shaken to the core and that has "doom" written all over it
because it lies under the judgment of God. We will often

get the balance between the two extremes of isolation and assimilation painfully wrong: but there is no other way if we are following in the footsteps of Jesus.

In the home-churches we will be able to help one another face up to the hidden feelings which are seared by any kind of rejection, such as Christians will receive when they take an unpopular stand on a particular issue in the local community. Nobody has been left unaffected by experiences of being rejected, often from early child-hood. The pain we associate with rejection, often subconsciously, often prevents us from entering into any situation where we know we will again be rejected. These are the realities of human experience which can be talked through, prayed over and ministered to in the fellowship of a home-church.

Once dealt with in the power of the Lord in such an accepting atmosphere, they become a source of strength in enabling the local church as a whole to face suffering and rejection over its witness to Jesus. We all long to be loved, not hated; accepted, not rejected; approved, not abused. Only the Spirit of God can bring healing and new courage to face the shame and suffering implicit in being faithful to Jesus. When he was abused, rejected and persecuted by everyone, he still found peace in the unchanging love of his Father God.

A vision of what the Church will one day be in the glory of heaven is an important context for appreciating God's vision for what he wants one particular local church to be. We have become a little ashamed of looking forward to the fullness of eternal life in heaven: it has seemed rather unfashionable in today's pragmatic world. The New Testament envisages every new day of discipleship, every fresh act of eucharistic worship, as anticipating the return of Christ in glory and "the marriage supper of the Lamb".[27] We are bidden to "seek the city which is to come"[28] not merely at odd occasions, such as the season of Advent, but as a regular habit of expectant faith. Only such eager anticipation will see us through the shame and suffering which are the calling of every Christian, treatment which our Father God turns to his own purposes in preparing us for life at home with him for ever in his unshakeable Kingdom.

We are called to suffer. We are also called to celebrate the rich grace of God in Jesus Christ, who remains "the same yesterday and today and for ever".[29] This high and all-absorbing calling can be fulfilled only through God himself – which is precisely the focus of the ascription of praise and prayer penned by the writer of that remarkable letter to the Hebrews: "Now may the God of peace who brought again from the dead our Lord Jesus, the great Shepherd of the sheep, by the blood of the eternal covenant, equip you with everything good that you may do his will, working in you that which is pleasing in his sight, through Jesus Christ; to whom be glory for ever and ever. Amen."[30]

References and notes

Biblical references are to the R.S.V. (Revised Standard Version) unless other versions are indicated – such as the A.V. (King James Authorised Version); T.E.V. ("Today's English" Version/ *Good News Bible*); and Phillips (*The New Testament in Modern English*, translated by J. B. Phillips, Collins, 1967).

Introduction
1   Prov. 29:18 (A.V.)
2   Michael Cassidy, *Bursting the Wineskins* (Hodder and Stoughton, 1983), pp. 68–69
3   Eph. 6:12

Chapter 1
1   Heb. 12:28
2   John Keble, "Sun of my soul, Thou Saviour dear", A. & M. No. 24
3   Charles Wesley, "Love Divine, all loves excelling", A. & M. No. 205
4   Heb. 12:22
5   Matt. 18:20 (A.V.)
6   Ps. 84:4 . . . 10
7   Ps. 22:3
8   Ps. 27:4
9   Ps. 35:18
10 Ps. 40:9–10. cf. Pss. 22:22, 25; 26:12; 66:13–16; 68:24–27
11 Ps. 42:4
12 Ps. 63:1
13 Ps. 63:2
14 Ps. 65:4
15 Ps. 68:26
16 1 Pet. 1:12
17 H. F. Lyte, "Praise, my soul, the King of Heaven", A. & M. No. 365
18 Rev. 5:11–12

19 Heb. 1:14
20 Heb. 12:23 (A.V.)
21 John 3:3ff
22 1 Cor. 14:16
23 cf. Luke 10:20; Rev. 13:8, 20:12 and 15
24 Heb. 12:23
25 B. McArthur
26 John 4:23–24
27 cf. Eph. 3:20
28 Eph. 3:21
29 Ps. 62:5
30 Eph. 3:10
31 Rev. 4:11. cf. Rev. 5:9, 11:17, 15:3
32 e.g. Rev. 5:11–14, 7:9–12
33 Col. 3:16
34 Eph. 5:19
35 Eph. 5:18
36 Heb. 12:23
37 John 21:15–17
38 John 21:15–17
39 Acts 2:46
40 Heb. 12:22 . . . 24
41 cf. Heb. 10:19ff
42 John 17:1, 11, 25
43 Heb. 12:23
44 Heb. 12:29
45 Heb. 12:18
46 Heb. 12:21
47 Matt. 12:36
48 Rev. 8:1
49 Gen. 2:2–3
50 H. Thielicke, *The Day the World Began* (James Clarke, 1964), pp. 103–6
51 ibid.
52 Hab. 2:20
53 Exod. 31:17
54 cf. Matt. 11:28–30 and Heb. 4:9
55 Heb. 13:15
56 Phil. 2:9–11
57 Rom. 12:1
58 Ps. 84:2
59 cf. Matt. 9:36, 14:14, 15:32; Mark 1:41, 6:34; Luke 7:13
60 2 Sam. 24:24
61 2 Chr. 20:21–22

Chapter 2

1   Heb. 13:1
2   John 13:34
3   John 13:35
4   John 13:1
5   John 13:14
6   1 Cor. 3:21–22
7   Luke 15:31
8   Matt. 20:26–28
9   John 13:6
10 John 13:20
11 Ps. 41:9
12 cf. Luke 22:15
13 Rom. 12:4–5
14 1 Cor. 12:27
15 John 13:1
16 Eph. 5:25
17 Phil. 1:9
18 Col. 1:4
19 1 Thess. 1:2–3
20 Rom. 5:5
21 I have written fully on home-churches in *The Church in the Home* (Marshall, Morgan and Scott, 1983)
22 1 John 3:14; cf. 5:1
23 cf. Acts 4:32ff
24 Acts 4:32
25 cf. Eph. 3:14–21
26 1 Sam. 18:1–4
27 Heb. 13:1

Chapter 3

1   Heb. 13:2
2   cf. Eph. 2:12
3   1 John 2:16 (T.E.V.)
4   1 Cor. 13:1
5   1 Cor. 13:2–3
6   cf. Rom. 1:14–17; 1 Cor. 9:19–23
7   Luke 4:38–41
8   Luke 5:17ff
9   Luke 5:27ff
10 Luke 7:36ff
11 Luke 11:35ff
12 Luke 14:1ff
13 Luke 8:39

14 Luke 8:40ff, 10:38ff, 19:1ff
15 Luke 9:1–2
16 Luke 9:4
17 Luke 10:5–9
18 Acts 5:42
19 Acts 9:43, 10:48
20 Acts 13:4–12
21 Acts 16:11–15
22 Acts 17:1ff
23 Acts 18:1ff
24 Acts 19:11–17
25 Acts 20:20–21
26 cf. 1 John 4:18
27 cf. John 3:16

Chapter 4
1 Heb. 13:3
2 1 John 2:3–6
3 Luke 5:12
4 Luke 17:11ff
5 Lev. 13 and 14
6 Lev. 13:45–46
7 Luke 5:27ff, 15:1–2, 19:1ff
8 Luke 15:1ff
9 Luke 7:38
10 John 4:9
11 Luke 9:54–55
12 Luke 10:30ff
13 Luke 18:35ff
14 Mark 8:22ff
15 cf. Luke 4:33ff, 4:41, 6:18, 7:21, 8:26ff, 9:37ff, 11:14ff, 13:10ff
16 Luke 1–3
17 Luke 8:1ff
18 Luke 4:38ff
19 Luke 7:11ff
20 Luke 7:36ff
21 Luke 8:43ff
22 Luke 10:38ff
23 Luke 21:1–4
24 Luke 23:49, 55–56; 24:1–12
25 Luke 2:41ff
26 Luke 8:40ff
27 Luke 9:37ff
28 Luke 9:46ff

29 Luke 10:21ff
30 Luke 17:1ff
31 Luke 18:15–17
32 Matt. 21:16
33 cf. chapter 1 of Michael Quoist's *Prayers of Life* (Gill and Macmillan, Dublin, 1963), pp. 3–4
34 cf. Jas. 1:27

Chapter 5
1 Heb. 13:4
2 Eph. 6:4
3 Howard Snyder, *Liberating the Church* (Marshalls, 1983), p. 129
4 Heb. 13:4
5 1 Thess. 4:3–8 (T.E.V.)

Chapter 6
1 Heb. 13:5–6 and 13:16
2 Col. 3:5; Eph. 5:5
3 cf. 1 Pet. 3:3–5
4 cf. 1 Tim. 4:4; Jas. 1:17
5 Luke 16:1–15
6 1 Tim. 6:10
7 Luke 18:25
8 cf. Luke 12:13–14, 14:12–24, 16:19–31, 17:22–37, 18:18–30, 19:1–10
9 Luke 16:8 (T.E.V.)
10 Luke 16:9
11 Luke 16:10–12
12 Luke 16:13
13 Mark 12:28–30. cf. Luke 10:25–28
14 Luke 4:7
15 Luke 4:8
16 Heb. 13:5
17 Heb. 13:6
18 Jas. 2:5
19 cf. Matt. 6:16
20 2 Cor. 8:2–5 (T.E.V.)
21 Luke 12:34
22 Luke 9:58
23 Matt. 8:19

Chapter 7

1   Heb. 13:7 and 13:17
2   Titus 1:9
3   cf. 1 Tim. 3:1–13; Titus 1:6–8
4   Titus 1:5
5   Acts 14:23
6   cf. 1 Pet. 5:1ff
7   cf. Luke 22:24ff
8   1 Cor. 16:15–16
9   See C. K. Barrett's commentary, *The First Epistle to the Corinthians* (A. and C. Black, 1968), p. 394
10 Eph. 4:7ff
11 The gist of this material on meetings is taken from an article in *The Times* on September 8th, 1983 by Winston Fletcher, the author of *Meetings, Meetings* (Michael Joseph, 1983)
12 Col. 3:15
13 John 14:27
14 Phil. 4:7
15 cf. Col. 3:12–17
16 Heb. 13:17
17 Hodder and Stoughton, 1983, pp. 166–7
18 1 Cor. 11:2–16; 1 Tim. 2:8–15
19 Heb. 13:8
20 Matt. 23:8–10
21 Matt. 23:11–12

Chapter 8

1   Heb. 13:9
2   Luke 12:32
3   1 Pet. 4:10 (A.V.)
4   Heb. 13:12
5   cf. Heb. 2:9ff, 4:14ff, 5:5ff, 7:23ff, 9:11ff, 10:5ff, 12:1–2
6   Luke 23:34
7   John 19:28
8   John 19:30
9   cf. 1 Cor. 12:28ff, Eph. 4:11ff
10 Jas. 3:1
11 Acts 6:1–6
12 Jas. 1:22–25
13 Luke 8:18
14 Col. 1:28–29
15 Acts 20:17ff
16 Acts 20:24
17 Acts 20:21

18   Acts 20:20
19   Acts 20:27
20   Acts 20:25
21   Acts 20:31
22   Acts 20:26
23   Acts 20:31
24   Acts 19:9 (margin)
25   Col. 3:16
26   I have written fully about this particular aspect of home-churches in chapter 5 of *The Church in the Home* (Marshall, Morgan and Scott, 1983)

Chapter 9

1   Heb. 13:12–14
2   Phil. 1:29
3   Luke 9:23
4   Luke 17:7–10 (T.E.V.)
5   cf. 1 Cor. 4:7
6   cf. Ps. 68:19 (A.V.)
7   1 Pet. 4:12. cf. 1 Pet. 1:6–7, 2:19ff, 3:14ff, 5:9–10
8   cf. Heb. 2:9ff, 5:7ff, 10:32ff, 12:3ff
9   Heb. 13:12–13
10   2 Cor. 4:12
11   2 Cor. 4:10
12   2 Cor. 4:11
13   Col. 1:24
14   2 Cor. 12:9
15   cf. Jas. 1:2 (Phillips)
16   John 15:18–21
17   cf. Rev. 18:1ff
18   Mark 12:37ff (A.V.)
19   Jas. 2:6–7
20   John 7:7
21   1 Pet. 2:20–21
22   1 Pet. 4:13
23   1 Pet. 4:14
24   Luke 6:22–23
25   Heb. 13:14
26   I have written at greater length on this topic in *Jesus or Britannia* (Grove Booklets, 1983)
27   cf. Rev. 19:9; 1 Cor. 11:26
28   Heb. 13:14
29   Heb. 13:8
30   Heb. 13:20–21